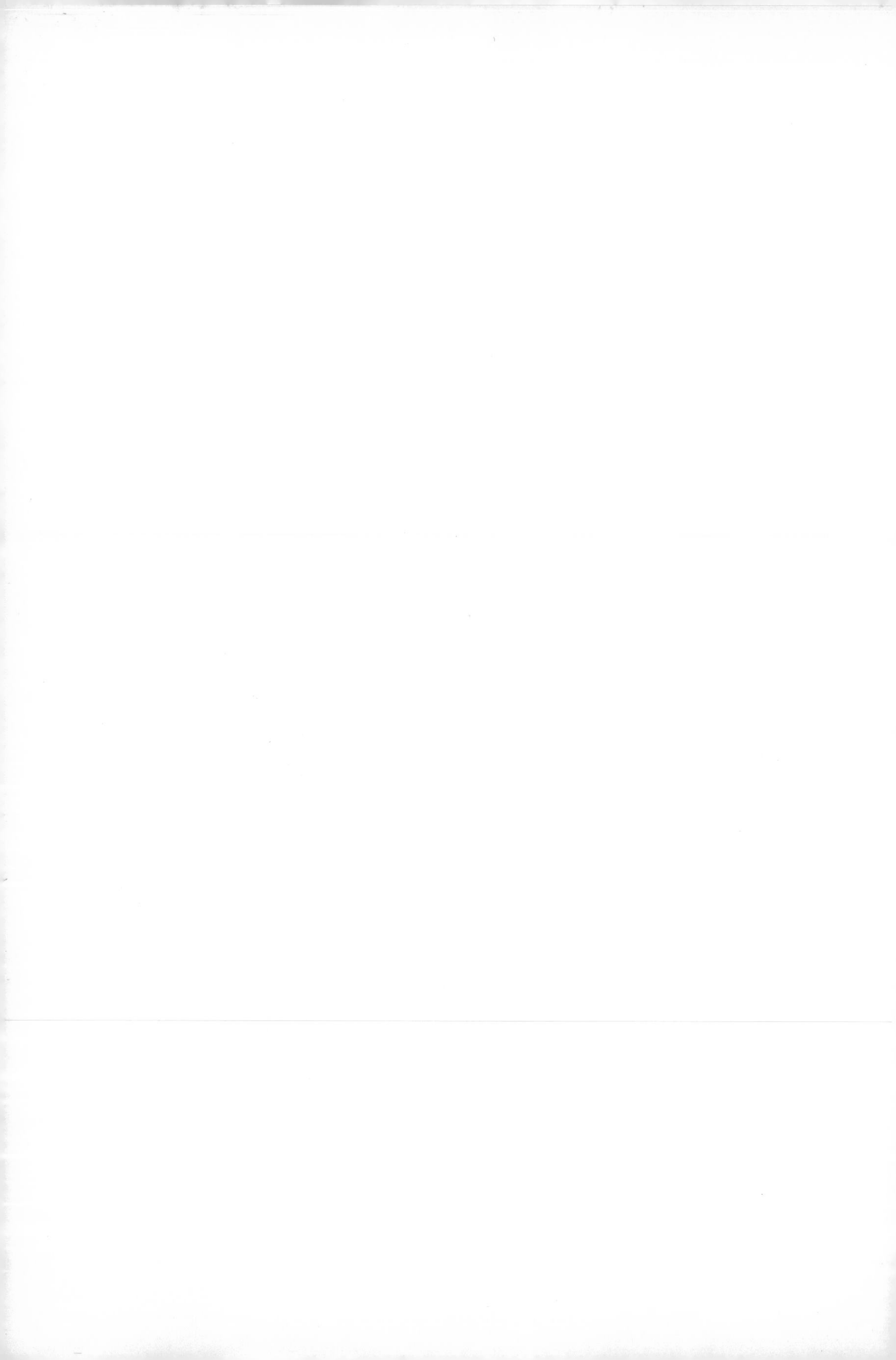

MORECAMBE and WIFE

For all the joy
For all the courage
For all the love –
Thank you

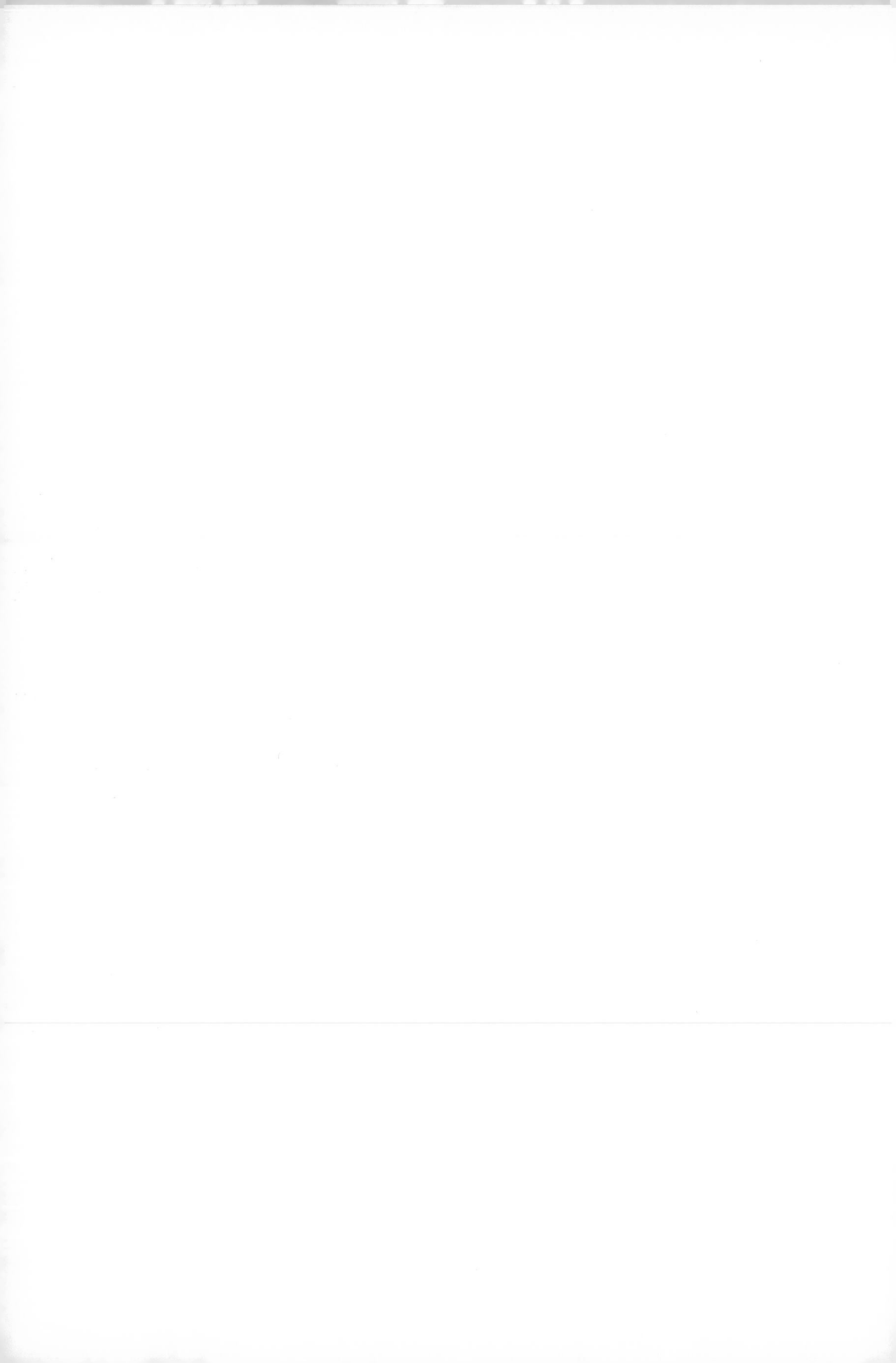

Contents

Photo Credits

The author and the publishers are grateful to the following for permission to reproduce copyright photographs in this book:

Bowman Photography page 146; *Daily Express* page 136; *Daily Mirror* pages 81, 153; *Daily Star* pages 170, 175 (top); *Derbyshire Advertiser* page 41 (top); R W Dudley page 64; *Echo and Post*, Hemel Hempstead pages 96, 140, 141; *Evening News* page 76; Jack Hickes page 95; Home Counties Newspapers page 88; Keystone Press page 107; J L Knowles page 77; Gary Morecambe page 164; The Press Association page 189; Keith Randall page 161 (bottom); Studio Cole page 121; *The Sun* page 125; D C Thomson pages 57 (bottom), 100. In some cases it has not been possible to ascertain the copyright holder and it is hoped that any such omissions will be excused.

Introduction

My one regret is that in our thirty-two years of married life Eric and I had so little time together, by ourselves. We met and were married within a few months and then almost immediately started a family. At first, with just one baby, I was able to travel with Eric from theatre to theatre, but for many years after I stayed at home raising our children, and relied on Eric being able to get home on a Sunday.

As the days of variety drew to an end and Eric and Ernie threw themselves into making a career in television, Eric was able to live at home. That was wonderful – a normal family life at last. But now the pressures were on.

In 1968 he had a massive heart attack. Nobody thought he would work again. He surprised everyone by bouncing back and he and Ernie went from strength to strength for another ten years. There was no end to their popularity, no end to their talent.

The damage to Eric's heart was permanent and it caught up with him in 1979. At Harefield Hospital he was told that he had the choice of open-heart surgery or a few weeks to live. 'What are you doing this afternoon?' he asked.

Again he bounced back into the demanding world of television. But now we started to look forward to retirement. In 1984 Eric was full of plans. He wanted to spend more time fishing and to see much more of his grandchildren. He had an ambition to drive from Boston to Florida, taking in the beauty of Maine and Vermont in the 'fall'. He wanted to see Rome and Venice. We were ready to relax and enjoy our own company in a way that we had almost never done before. Then in May he went to Tewkesbury to appear in a Sunday concert. He collapsed as he left the stage, and died.

This book tells the story, and is a celebration of the life we shared together. Eric always said what an extraordinary amount we had packed into our lives. If only we could have been granted a few more years.

1
Bartholomew and Bartlett

It was Eric's idea. Minutes after we were introduced he said to someone who knew us both – as though it was a statement of fact – that this was the girl he would marry. It was as sudden as that. Later he said there should be a plaque on the stage of the Edinburgh Empire, where it all happened, saying 'Eric Morecambe Fell Here'.

For my part I wasn't especially pleased to be there. I was struggling to get ahead in show business – a business I had joined almost accidentally. I had no professional training, only the confidence of youth, the willingness to work hard and a certain amount of natural talent and looks.

Ever since I was a little girl I had loved dancing, singing, music and acting – anything from tap dancing to Shakespeare. Because of the war, I was one of that generation of wasted youngsters whose education more or less fizzled out. We were living in Tidworth, Hampshire, and that was where I spent my last years at school. I did well in class, but left school at sixteen without any qualifications and went to work in a local garage. I taught myself shorthand and typing, and as I learnt how to run the office my boss put me on to answering the correspondence of other businesses which he owned. Then I won a competition while I was away on holiday; the prize was the chance to go to London and train as a fashion model. Suddenly my life was drastically changed.

I moved up to London and went to stay with friends. The training course lasted only a few weeks and I felt very uncertain of myself in this strange new world. In many ways fashion modelling was a crazy career to have tried to go in for because there were already too many

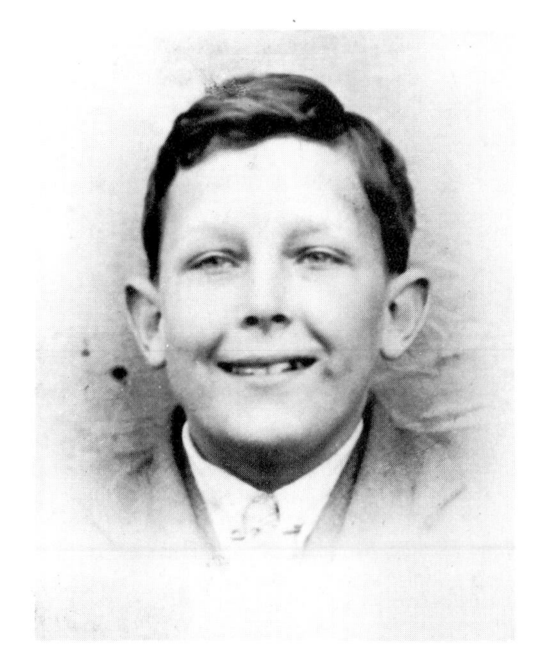

TOP LEFT Eric all smartened up to have his school photograph taken. TOP RIGHT This was a snapshot taken in Burma of my mother, brother and me. BOTTOM LEFT Alan and me try our hand at fishing. BOTTOM RIGHT Alan and me.

girls who couldn't get work. The trouble was, I now had a real desire to succeed – and so I resolved to stay, and moved in with my grandparents in Coulsdon, and commuted to London every day.

I had enough sense to realize that I would starve instantly if I tried to earn a living as a freelance model – the glamorous side of the business – so while I did a few engagements which gave me some very necessary experience, I became a permanent model with a tailoring and design firm. This involved doing various other jobs in the showroom and working as a house model when needed. During the lunch breaks, still burning with ambition, I would dash along to some of the agencies to see if there was something more interesting which I could apply for. No wonder I had no difficulty in keeping

ABOVE Can this really be Eric as a toddler? His legs didn't stay chubby like that for long! RIGHT 'A musical family'. Sadie and George with young Eric.

slim! All those flights of stairs on tube stations, taken at great speed, with no time for eating more than a sandwich.

From out of the blue, a few other models and I were offered the chance to audition for a new musical – a stage show – and I grabbed it. The show was to open in Manchester and then move to London. That first taste of the theatre captivated me and I had a very happy time. From then on I was determined to stay in show business if I possibly could. Going from one precarious career to another!

The musical over, I began touring the country in variety shows. It wasn't an easy life – short on money and home comforts – and much harder for a girl than a feller. What I really wanted was to be a singer, but unfortunately nobody wanted to listen! Then in the early summer of 1952 a girl appearing in the show at the Empire Theatre, Edinburgh went down with appendicitis and was taken to hospital. A replacement was needed right away to fill in for a few weeks until the girl recovered. Lew and Leslie Grade knew of me from previous work and asked if I would like the job. The pay was good, even though the walk-on part needed little talent. I was anyway becoming rather depressed at my lack of progress; also, I had never been to the lovely city of Edinburgh before, so that was something to look forward to. The show was there for one week, then travelled on to the next date. On the same bill were Eric and Ernie – comedians I had frequently heard of but never seen.

We met on a Monday morning at bandcall. The routine was that everyone in the show arrived at the theatre and put their band parts on the stage. It was organized on a basis of first come, first served, and one by one the performers went through their music with the resident band. As it happened Eric and Ernie were doing their bandcall when I arrived. Also in the theatre was Anita, a very pleasant American girl who knew Eric and Ernie. She introduced us, and Eric was hooked.

Before that moment I suppose I had thought 'love at first sight' was little more than a convenient device which writers used to make their stories go with a swing. I had certainly never been a victim of it, and I found the experience fairly strange. Eric, however, was completely certain in his own mind and very persuasive. In no time at all he had asked me out for coffee. By the end of the week, when we temporarily parted company, he had proposed, and then he went on asking me about once a fortnight until I said yes. We were married on 11 December that year.

For those of you who believe in fate, there were enough similarities in our backgrounds to suggest that we might indeed be 'destined for one another'. To begin with, he was called John Eric Bartholomew and my name was Joan Bartlett. Not only are John and Joan the same name, Bartholomew and Bartlett also have the same origins. In the Middle Ages, Bartholomew was a popular surname, and Bartlett is derived directly from it. In addition, as we soon discovered, we both came from seaside towns beginning with 'M': Eric had been brought up in Morecambe and my parents had settled in Margate. These were just simple coincidences. Far more impressive was Eric's absolute certainty at that first meeting.

At various times in his life Eric took big decisions quickly, going on intuition, and he had the happy knack of 'getting it right'. That day in Edinburgh he instinctively knew that I was the one for him. This meant, in terms of our characters, that I would be a suitable foil to his own nature, which was, impatient and unpractical, with no liking for the everyday problems of life. If he had married someone like himself, it would have been a disaster, or so he often told me in the years to come. Without really analysing it, he knew that he needed someone who would give him confidence and be a calm influence. How anyone can work all that out in a single glance is beyond me; but that is what Eric did, and the pursuit was on.

'Can you come for a coffee?' I can't remember the precise words, or what else we said on that first day. I do know that Eric made me laugh and was always a master at getting his own way, which is possibly why I agreed to go out with him. I certainly wasn't looking for anyone, in fact I already had a boyfriend, and after coffee I remember towing Eric around the shops while I tried to find a birthday present for this other man. In the end I bought a silver tankard, and from that day Eric could never look at a tankard without reminding me of that occasion – a blow to his masculine pride.

Whatever reservations I may have had about being pursued by a young, eager Northern comedian, I had no doubt that Eric and Ernie would be stars. Apart from a short break during the war they had been on the road together since their early teens – 'Two boys of fourteen with spots telling jokes about their wives,' was how Eric once put it – and by the time they reached the Edinburgh Empire in 1952 they had worked their way up the bill to 'second top'.

Both the boys owed a great deal to Eric's mother, Sadie Bartholomew. She was a wonderful, humorous and determined woman who had toured with them when they were teenagers, arranging their bookings and digs, generally keeping a watchful eye on them, and in Eric's case making sure he didn't spend all his money as soon as he had earned it. In the early years, when they didn't always have work, there was always a welcome for them in Morecambe with Eric's mum and dad. When they reached the age of eighteen they were called up for war service. Ernie was the first to go, and he joined the Merchant Navy and worked on coasters, then Eric spent eleven months as a Bevin Boy down a coal mine in Accrington. He was classified A1 at his first medical, and when they sent him home in less than a year he was C3. This was to prove the beginning of his heart problems, and for about a year he had to take life very quietly. He met up with Ernie again quite accidentally. They ran into each other in the street and decided to team up again.

In the early years after the war, Eric and Ernie had a tough time establishing themselves, and bookings were thin on the ground. But despite the long periods of unemployment, Sadie was always supportive and Eric's dad, George, was both patient and self-sacrificing, having resigned himself to the fact that his wife was going to spend a lot of time away from home in order to be with the boys. One booking was for a doomed outfit called Lord John Sanger's Circus and Variety. They managed to get odd weeks in places like the Barry Docks, Cardiff and the Palace, Walthamstow and they filled in here and there with ENSA. The two of them lasted one week at the Windmill Theatre, and then they were hired by Reggie Dennis's touring show, *Front Page Personalities*, for £27.10s a week between them. This show lasted for almost a year, during which time they polished their act and gradually began to win favourable notices in the local papers.

Towards the end of 1950, Eric and Ernie signed a sole agency agreement with Frank Pope, who fixed bookings for them with the

Moss Empire theatres. These ranked as Number One variety theatres, whereas before they had mainly worked in the Second Division. Now they were in regular, demanding work, performing six days a week and travelling on the Sunday to the next venue. In December they went into pantomime until about Easter; a little later in their careers they also appeared in summer shows at one of the big seaside resorts. Until television took over a pattern established itself of: panto, touring in variety, summer show, then back to touring, plus, for good measure, a lot of radio broadcasts which they usually did on a Sunday.

That was the annual ritual for performers at their level in the dying years of variety. Television was somewhere in the wings, waiting to pounce and transform their lives completely, but as yet it

RIGHT Eric Bartholomew – almost a professional!
BELOW This is how Eric was dressed when he used to sing the song 'I'm not all there'. I still have the prop lollipop, as Sadie and George kept it over the years along with the first pair of shoes, first top hat etc.

Eric and Ernie at the start of their career in show business as a double act.

played little part in their thoughts. Eric and Ernie were very popular on the variety circuit, and enormous fun to be with. They were witty, quick, and had such youthful vitality that they made friends wherever they appeared. Their dressing-room was often filled with other artistes or visitors who had come to call and enjoy their company. You could always hear the sound of laughter coming through their dressing-room door.

Eric was very content to be second top of the bill. It was a question of responsibility. If a show failed to bring in the audiences, it was said to be the fault of the star who was top of the bill. He or she had to shoulder all the blame. Of course, they took the praise if the show succeeded, but Eric was happy at that stage in his career to shelter from any possible repercussions and at the same time have his name

Two very young newcomers to the world of show biz.

in nice thick print along the bottom of the bill. That way he enjoyed the kudos, because his name already meant something in the business, but he did not have to carry the can. Nevertheless, he was ambitious and wanted to get to the top. He always had that ultimate goal in mind.

Eric and Ernie were still young men, barely in their mid-twenties, and in those days overnight success was almost unknown. However talented you might be, the only way to become a big star was to work and gain experience. If you were good enough you might just make it. Eric and Ernie had always been tremendous workers, and they had something special about them. Now they just needed some luck and a little bit of extra confidence.

In the early part of his career, Eric had benefited from the backing of his mother, Sadie, and she had enjoyed the years spent encouraging him. Then, at the time of his twenty-first birthday she wrote him a letter. It began with some details about his presents – which included twenty-one bars of rock! – and then went on:

> 'I want to thank you for being a good boy to us and not bringing us any trouble. I know at times you have thought me hard but I have had to do it for your own benefit. Now you are your own boss and I sincerely hope you have learned a little from my nagging. I don't want to be sentimental but I just want you to know how we both have loved you and tried to do our best for you. As you know we always wanted you to have only the best, and though now to the world you are a man, to us you will always be our baby (so don't get any big ideas). From now on I do not interfere with whatever you do, but if you want advice well of course we will be there. . . .'

The special bond between Sadie and her only child comes out very clearly in the letter. And although in no sense was she pushing him suddenly out into the world and leaving him to get on with it, I think she did feel that with Eric no longer a child her role as mother, minder and manager was coming to an end. Eric said to me from the very beginning that he had to have a woman in his life. In 1952 he had reached a stage where he was very restless. The family home in Morecambe was still his base, and he returned there whenever he could, but the life of a touring comedian left little time for family visits, and in any case Eric needed a new kind of companion. One Monday morning in Edinburgh he spotted me, and there and then decided that all his problems were solved!

So who was I, this Joan Bartlett who was suddenly the centre of attraction in Eric's life? As far as my own career was concerned I was, as I have mentioned, something of an accident of show business. I had my ambitions to succeed as a solo artiste, and in the period before I met Eric I had spent months preparing and rehearsing an act. The clothes alone cost £180, a lot of money then, but the demand for female singing acts was distinctly on the low side and I was unknown and untried.

Before setting my sights on being a singer, I made a living touring in shows as a soubrette. It is not a word you hear today, and it probably died along with the old style of variety show, but in those days a soubrette was an all-rounder who did all kinds of bits and pieces. She would go on and do a few lines with the comic or work in a sketch, she might sing a song if necessary, and do a bit of dancing. It was a very useful way for a relative newcomer like me to gain some all-round experience, but when I tried to move up to something bigger I ran into problems.

Goodness knows what made me press on with my show-business ambitions. There was nothing in my background to encourage it. It would have been far more suitable if I had taken up nursing or teaching. But the war had made life unpredictable for a lot of families, including mine; it had filled the thoughts of everyone, blotting out the future and ideas of training and getting qualifications – particularly for a girl. It was assumed that girls would anyway soon get married and not want a career – a very different outlook from today.

My father had been in the Royal Army Medical Corps for a number of years, and this meant that as a family we travelled around a great deal. I spent part of my early childhood in Burma, then we moved to London, and when war broke out I was in one of those first waves of evacuees who were sent away to the country with a name tag around their necks. I had my brother Alan with me. Sadly, being evacuated didn't work out for us. We were most unhappy in the place we were billetted, and only too glad to be soon reunited with our mother.

Then we joined my father in Tidworth, Hampshire, but as soon as we were all together again he was sent off to Burma where he had an extremely hard war. When he came back, he was shattered – both mentally and physically – and for health reasons he was advised to go and live by the coast. He retired as a captain in the Medical Corps, and he and my mother bought a house in Cliftonville, Margate. Shortly afterwards my brother, who in the meantime had joined an Airborne Division, returned from his period of service and got married. He had no career to go to, and so they all went into business together, selling the house in Cliftonville to put up the money for a pub-hotel called the Bull's Head. My father had made a good recovery

LEFT I was living in Tidworth at this time and had started my first job. BELOW I only entered the Miss Margate contest on the spur of the moment for a little bit of fun, little dreaming I would end up representing the town for the Miss Kent contest.

by then, and my mother was always a very attractive, active lady – they needed to be active because the business they had taken on was run-down and required a great deal of hard work to set it on its feet. The partnership with my brother worked well, and as a result my family have stayed in that line of business ever since – though Dad has long since passed away.

Eric was very attentive towards me during that week in Edinburgh. Each morning everyone in the show would call at the theatre to collect any mail that had arrived. Then we would go out and have

My dad taken in uniform during the war.

coffee in the town and lunch back at our digs. In the afternoon the cinema was the favourite place to go. The most important thing to remember was to be at the theatre on time – usually around 5pm – and then we got ready for the two evening performances.

After work it would be late, and people went back to their digs for a meal and bed. Because of this strange timetable, one always tried to get proper theatrical digs with a landlady who understood our special needs. We lived to that pattern for six days a week, and on the Sunday, if you had a booking to go to, moved on to the next town. If you didn't have a booking, you went back to your parents or your own home base and waited for the phone to ring.

It was not a particularly comfortable life, but that is how people like Eric and Ernie chose to live for year after year. Once they were in regular work, they never stopped. They worked the whole time, never dreaming of turning down an engagement, never taking holidays like ordinary people, and certainly never getting a break at traditional times like Christmas, because they would then be hard at work doing two or more performances a day in pantomime.

After Edinburgh, Eric and I went our separate ways to appear on different bills, but it so happened that we were booked in the same show in several other towns, and so we did get together again and I began to learn a little more about this thin, humorous man who kept proposing to me. One day we found, by a complete coincidence, that Eric was booked to appear for a week in Margate – my parents' town – while I was going to be in Morecambe – his town. Eric said immediately: 'Look, if you want somewhere to go and stay, please go and see my mother and father and they'll be glad to put you up.'

My parents, brother and sister-in-law were by then running the Bull's Head in Margate, and so it was only natural to suggest that Eric and Ernie stayed there. Which they did, along with half the Billy Cotton Band who had nowhere else to go.

After that, Eric and I kept in regular touch at weekends, and had countless phone conversations in between times. Just arranging to get together involved schedules that would make many people wince with pain and give up. But not Eric. If possible he would travel after his last show on the Saturday night or else catch a train early on Sunday morning to wherever I was. We would have a few hours together on the Sunday, and he would continue to the next town where he was working. This was not only difficult to do, it was also extremely tiring. The railways at the weekend still seemed to be living up to that wartime slogan: 'Is Your Journey Really Necessary?' But when you're young and in love it doesn't seem to matter.

Part of the time I was in London looking for more work, and then it was usually easier for Eric to reach me. A lot depended on which theatres he was playing, and of course they might be anywhere from Scotland to Swansea. Once or twice I did the travelling. That was the kind of courtship we had – a little frenzied and all too brief.

Towards the end of the year, we got engaged, and one of the essential differences in our characters came to the surface. Although my time in show business had been difficult, I had always believed in 'spend a little, save a little', so I always tried to put something by whenever it came in. Eric, on the other hand, had little interest in counting his pennies, with the result that he never had anything in reserve. He borrowed the money for our engagement ring from his mother. She was happy to lend it, but she couldn't resist saying: 'I don't know what she sees in our Eric. It can't be his money!'

The ring was a beautiful solitaire diamond, which reflected Eric's 'nothing-but-the-best' side. Now his campaign was nearly won, and he completed it with one of those desperate suggestions which is the mark of the true showman. He rang up and told me that he and Ernie would shortly be having a few days off – an unheard-of thing but this was because they were due in London to do a radio broadcast from the Palladium with Tessie O'Shea on Monday 12 December. That meant we could get married on the Sunday, couldn't we, travel up to London for a combined honeymoon and broadcast, and catch a train to Sheffield!

In its mad way it all made sense. Eric and Ernie never did have any spare time, and they did have to be in Sheffield immediately after the London broadcast because they were booked for a pantomime season at the Theatre Royal. I agreed, and launched into one of the most frantic few days of my life.

I rang my mother. Could she organize a wedding for us at such short notice? She said she would, although her reply was a trifle guarded:

'Yes, dear,' she said, adding, 'if that is what you want.'

I contacted the vicar of St John's Church in Margate, and he agreed to marry us by special licence on the Sunday. The printers were hustled into producing invitations at very short notice. The guests, for the same reason, would be in short supply! The reception, fortunately, wasn't a problem because my parents were in the hotel trade and so could put all that together quickly.

My mother and I travelled up to London from Margate to find a wedding outfit for me. Not the dreamed-of white bridal gown, just something smart and simple. In London we were confronted with not only a pea-soup fog but shops devoid of anything really suitable in the way of a dress or shoes. As there was such little time I settled for what was available.

How does one explain to any young person today that the shops really did have very little to sell? Rationing and recovering from the war lasted for many years. And so did those pea-soup fogs, when you couldn't see a hand in front of you. Thank goodness they are in the past.

The other problem we had was getting round Eric's mother, Sadie. Only the previous week she had put an announcement in the *Morecambe Visitor*, the local newspaper, to tell everyone in that part of the world that we had become engaged. Now, all of a sudden, we were getting married!

'Why rush things?' she said. 'How disappointing not to wait and have a big white wedding.'

Then there was the journey to consider. She and George, Eric's father, were in Morecambe ... but the wedding was to be down in

Margate. In the South. Oh, no. It was too much. Too far. Too soon. People she had never even met!

For a while Sadie refused to come to the wedding, and Eric had to be at his most persuasive and diplomatic before she gave in and agreed to come. In the end, of course, when they did get to Margate they were made extremely welcome by my family – who are very easy people – and they had a marvellous time. They stayed at the hotel and thoroughly enjoyed the whole thing. It was a real holiday for them and they talked about it for weeks after.

Apart from a spell of thick fog which came down over the whole country until the Saturday – and gave Eric a few frights because he always had a mania for being punctual – the wedding passed off according to plan. I only kept him waiting a short while at the church, and a few minutes after 3 o'clock on 11 December 1952 we

LEFT Fancy us having a cake like this when we only planned the wedding eight days previously! Sadie and George all smiles in the background. OPPOSITE So this is what a family group looks like! The Bartholomews are outnumbered by the Bartletts. Both mums are in the front row either side of us, with our dads immediately behind them. My grandparents and an aunt, uncle and cousin are also in the back row. Alan and Pam are at either end of the front row.

were pronounced Morecambe & Wife.

Ernie was best man – although he did look a little shattered at the speed with which his boyhood partner had whisked himself away to marry a third party; but soon afterwards Ernie married Doreen, whom he had known for some years already, and the group settled down to a new pattern of living and working.

The real comedian at our wedding was the photographer. Admittedly, my mother had to find someone at short notice, but I have never discovered where this man came from – unless it was the promenade. He had the full works – a massive camera on a tripod which might have done service in the Crimean War, and an all-enveloping black cloth which he disappeared under for minutes at a stretch. It was the sort of equipment Eric and Ernie would use in a sketch for laughs. Although he made Eric laugh, I can't say we were

bowled over by the resulting set of group photographs. They were black and white, of course, and much less glamorous than the pictures we are used to seeing today. Many years later, a man came up to Eric and said:

'You don't know me. But my father took your wedding photographs.'

Eric said he nodded and smiled at him, and tried very hard not to say: 'There's no answer to that!'

2
Careless Rapture

Our honeymoon was not so much a honeymoon as a running rehearsal for the broadcast with Tessie O'Shea. The show meant a lot to Eric and he desperately wanted it to be good, so we spent our wedding evening at the Cumberland Hotel going through his lines!

Next day, the broadcast over, we travelled up to Sheffield for the pantomime season and moved into the coldest, dreariest digs I can remember. I'd been used to a comfortable home background, with my parents or grandparents, and although by now I'd had lots of experience of touring in variety, and stayed in more poor digs than good ones, this place came as a big disappointment. We also had to contend with the fact that Sheffield in those days was not the city it is today. Dense smogs descended and blotted out the daylight, and everyone seemed to live in an eternal grey-yellow atmosphere, that winter being one of the worst on record. We suffered a combination of snow, sleet and smog, and always there was no escape from the biting cold. Of course, everyone was suffering, not just us, but it wasn't the most romantic way to start our married life. As Eric would say: 'Life isn't Hollywood, it's Cricklewood.'

Off we went in search of somewhere better and eventually found a much more comfortable place, run by a pleasant, understanding landlady who rented us her front room which she had turned into a bedsitter for theatricals. It had a three-piece suite and a bed in it, so was fairly full of furniture, but best of all it had a good open fire which the landlady conscientiously looked after for us. We bought our own food and she cooked it. In the morning she would light the fire and get our breakfast ready, and in the evening she cooked us a late supper after the show.

Soon, to our great surprise, I found that I was pregnant. It certainly wasn't planned. Eric said it must have been the cold digs! We were thrilled at the prospect of becoming parents, and at the time we never thought of the difficulties that starting a family so soon would present.

Life could still have settled down to something approaching normal but, unfortunately, I began to suffer dreadful bouts of morning sickness which lasted until the middle of the afternoon. When Eric was at the theatre, I would spend most of the time in the dressing-room. Invariably, dressing-rooms were bleak little rooms and so everyone would take pains to pretty them up. After all, this was 'home' for many weeks, where most hours of the day would be spent. A kettle and cups and saucers were first on the list. After the matinees it felt like sheer luxury to brew up, and we would enjoy a few 'goodies' that I had shopped for to tide us over until supper, which was always a very late meal.

To help me through this awful sickness stage, Eric packed me off every so often to recuperate at his parents' house in Morecambe. We had mixed feelings about these partings, but as soon as I got to the coast and could breathe the sea air, the sickness disappeared and I would feel fit and healthy. I never stayed for more than a few days because I was bursting to get back again to Eric. Each time I returned, back came the sickness, so we could only put it down to the foggy atmosphere in Sheffield (which, I'm glad to say, has long since been removed from the city).

The pantomime played to full houses for three months, and then we went on tour in variety. The opening date was at Norwich, and followed up with the boys' first big London West End break – two weeks at The London Palladium. Afterwards it was back to reality with the usual round of travelling from town to town. I did find those Sunday journeys from one venue to the next a bit of an ordeal. The straightforward journeys were fine, but often there would be two or three changes, with lots of waiting about in between – not ideal for someone expecting her first baby. One week, I remember, we had to travel down to Portsmouth; the very next week we were due in Leeds. Ernie and Doreen had graduated to travelling by car, but Eric hadn't learnt to drive so it was still good old British Railways for us.

Eric and I were both lucky to be blessed with good families who would always help us if they could – and what could be more convenient than to have one lot in the North and one in the South. For the time being there was no point in us setting up home anywhere. We couldn't afford to buy a place, and what was the good of renting a home that we'd never have time to live in. The baby was due in mid-September, and we were well aware that these few months of freedom would soon come to an end.

Both our families understood the position, and they were happy to offer us a base whenever we needed it, and somewhere to leave our possessions. We saved hard for the future – as well as repaying Sadie in instalments for the engagement ring! We were now saving for a car and Eric's driving lessons.

Sadie, George and I quickly got to know each other better. I even found I could understand my father-in-law! George's accent was very Northern, or so it seemed, when we first met. But soon I reached a stage where I was no longer conscious that he and I spoke with different accents. The relationship between a mother and the wife of her only son can be extremely delicate, but Sadie and I soon developed a respect and liking for each other. I'm sure that each of us had shortcomings in the other's eyes, but it only requires a little tact and tolerance to bridge the differences. I can never understand this business of people taking umbrage with their in-laws and often refusing to be on speaking terms. Family life is complicated enough without all that nonsense.

The more I travelled around the countryside the more I actually enjoyed the differences between North and South. Show business in the 'fifties and 'sixties still had its own traditional frontiers which dated back to music hall days. Comedians, for instance, were distinctly classified as either Northern or Southern, and were not expected to succeed outside their own territory. What finally broke all barriers was television. I always remember watching the first episode of *Coronation Street* with Eric. Our joint verdict was: 'They must be mad, showing this in London. It'll never catch on!'

It took a few years to come about, but eventually people in the South realized that they understood and laughed at Northern comics and Northern humour, and vice versa. There really was no division, despite what people in the theatre had believed for all those years. But television was a good teacher, and entertainment became a daily part of life. As time went by, television brought many Northern comics down South, where, if all went well, they settled. This eventually happened to Eric and Ernie. You could always tell that Eric was from the North by his accent, and, of course, knowing his name could help. But then, as he often said: 'My real name's not Morecambe, you know – it's Blackpool!'

Eric and Ernie were booked to do the next summer season in Blackpool, so that was where we would be when the baby arrived. We rented a small house in the town and lived there throughout those summer months, just like any other ordinary young couple. I began to bloom, as expectant mothers often do, and felt fighting fit. Each Sunday we would go to Eric's parents in Morecambe. We had to, or we'd never have heard the last of it! They loved having us, and Sadie seemed to cook for a whole army. Then, nearer my time, we moved in with them and each day Eric drove backwards and forwards to the theatre. Yes, we were now the proud owners of an Austin Hereford; Eric had learnt to drive during the summer season, and passed his test first time.

I had always wanted to have the baby at home, that is, at Sadie and George's home. Unfortunately, I was blissfully ignorant of the fact that it is a lot easier to have a first baby in hospital.

It was a long and difficult birth. I went into labour on the morning of Sunday 13 September. Although I was in a lot of pain, nothing seemed to be happening so we didn't send for the midwife until the next morning. She predicted the baby would arrive by noon and be a boy. This was a relief to Eric as well as me. For my part, everything that happened was new and alarming; as for Eric, he seemed on the point of a nervous breakdown, and he certainly didn't want to leave for the theatre until the baby was born.

Midday came and went with no sign of the baby. The hours dragged on painfully and now Eric had to leave – or miss the first show. He was quite sure by that time that something was wrong.

He and Ernie were at the Winter Gardens Theatre, and Alan Jones – father of the singer Jack Jones – was top of the bill. I don't think

Eric gave the greatest performance of his life that night, but he struggled through somehow.

At long last, around seven o'clock in the evening, I gave birth to a baby daughter weighing a little over six pounds. She was fine, and so was I in an utterly exhausted way; Sadie and George were nervous wrecks, but Sadie managed to telephone the news to the theatre. Eric was on stage at the time, and soon he noticed that the conductor in

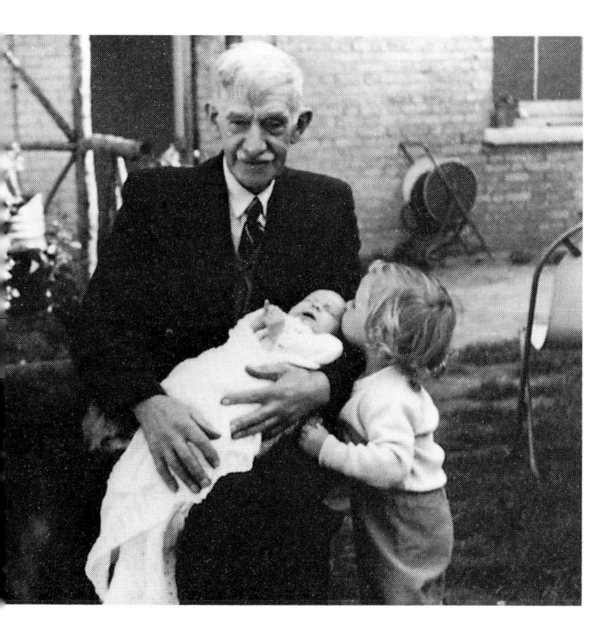

ABOVE My grandfather with the new arrival, Gail, and his other great-grandchild Clive.
RIGHT Two smashing ladies – mother and grandmother.

the orchestra was pulling strange faces at him; no, mouthing a message! He made out the words: 'It's a GIRL . . . a GIRL.'

He and Ernie finished their performance, and Eric was given permission to leave the theatre before the finale. Home he dashed and, as the finale ended, Alan Jones announced: 'Ladies and gentlemen, I am thrilled to be able to tell you that Eric's wife, Joan, has just given birth to a six-month-old baby girl!'

3
Running Wild

Eric never wanted to drive, but now there were three of us. The arrival of our tiny baby daughter, Gail, meant that in future the Morecambes would have to travel up and down the country with something like double the baggage they had been used to.

Gail was a lovely baby with blonde hair (though not much of it!), and was chubby and healthy from the beginning. We were delighted with her but it was now dawning on us just how much equipment you need for one small infant – and how on earth do you fit it all into a car when you are on tour?

We didn't need to take one of those great springy baby carriages with us, though we couldn't resist buying one. We decided on a compact, collapsible type for touring; Gail could also make do with a carrycot instead of a full-sized cot until she outgrew it. But for the most part it wasn't easy to find ways of travelling light. One good thing was that breast-feeding saved all the bother of tins of baby food and sterilizing apparatus, as well as proving a great comfort to Gail on long, tedious journeys. And, as Eric would say: 'It comes in such cute containers!'

Our first big journey was from Morecambe to Margate for Gail's christening, after which she and I would spend a little time there. She was about three weeks old, and we had arranged for the christening to be at the church where we were married. Eric looked forward to the journey with alarm. He had a right to be apprehensive. There he was, a novice driver, about to transport his wife and baby across three hundred miles of unknown roads, in an age when motorways didn't exist. The prospect of all those busy A roads didn't appeal

Our first car complete with an overworked roof-rack.

to his spirit of adventure at all, and so we contacted the Automobile Association and asked them to send us an itinerary which followed the B roads. Not only would it be safer, it would make the ride a lot prettier! We would also miss out all the town centres, which in those days were a regular obstacle to every long journey. You had to go through the whole lot, and that could take ages, particularly when you hit a rush hour.

A big document arrived from the AA, was duly studied, and a few days later we set off. It took us two days to reach Margate, staying overnight in Huntingdon to break the journey. Funnily enough, we have since got to know that area quite well, because many years later we went into the hotel business there with my brother, but in 1953 it was foreign soil. Anyway, the journey passed uneventfully, the views were lovely, and when we got to Margate we were welcomed with open arms by my family. Eric said it took several minutes for me to prise his knuckles loose from the steering-wheel. Later, when I too learned to drive, I could appreciate that we had achieved something special with that journey. It certainly helped to give Eric a lot of confidence.

Meanwhile, with the summer season ended, it was back to touring. Gail and I were to stay in Margate for part of the time and not always be on the move with Eric. It all worked out surprisingly well.

Gail was three months old when we returned to Sheffield for Eric's second season of pantomime there. That year, at least, we had a house to go to. Sadie had been very good. She had gone across from Morecambe and found a place for us to rent for the three months. The house itself was adequate and we were glad to have it. There were only two drawbacks. The first was the position of the house (on top of a steep hill) and the second was the weather. For the second year running we had one of those dreadful cold winters which go on and on and make you think there will never be another spring. For weeks we had thick snow; we couldn't believe it could be so bad two years in succession.

At times the weather and the steep journey to and from the house combined to make going to the shops more like an expedition through the Himalayas. Pushing a pram downhill to go to the shops wasn't so bad, but just try getting it back up! I can remember feeling quite desperate on more than one occasion, as I took one step forward and slipped back two. Gail would lie serenely in the pram, all nice and snug, quite unaware that her mother was beginning to wonder if they would ever get home.

The other running battle I waged was in the house, trying to get it warm. That was a challenge I usually lost. Central heating was still a distant dream. We had a boiler and you fetched the coal in a bucket from the cellar. In the sitting room there was an open fire, but I can't remember being in that house without seeing my own breath. You had to be made of hardy stuff actually to have a bath and it was far less painful to stay dirty! Gail was all right with her little enamel bath perched in front of the fire, the towels nicely warming. I'd have willingly changed places with her!

Each morning I'd get up about 6.30 am, when my lovely little human alarm clock told me she wanted attention, and then I'd have my first battle of the day with the boiler – though I cannot say my eyes were actually open at that time. Going to bed so late – and with sleep being somewhat disturbed for the odd 'milk-on-tap' feed – didn't make one feel at one's best first thing.

It was no longer possible for me to join Eric at the theatre during the evening but, although I was rather lonesome, the time didn't drag because there always seemed to be so much to do. Sadie had told me that once I had a baby I'd wonder what on earth I'd done with my time before. And it was true. Everything took longer then of course with no washing machine or other labour-saving devices. There were loads of towelling nappies to boil and all those beautiful little woollens we loved to dress Gail in which needed careful hand-washing. Eric's socks were darned and my nylon stockings painstakingly mended when they laddered. Shirts were hand-washed and ironed.

How times have changed. When I think of the effort that went into keeping us smart – and smart we were – it seems like another world. I'm glad, though, that young mums today, like Gail herself, have far more free time to devote to other interests and hobbies outside the home. I sometimes wonder at the perverseness of human nature. For years the shops had remained devoid of attractive clothes and so we all went to great lengths to look pretty and make the most of what was available. Now the shops fairly bulge with gorgeous temptations but most of the youngsters seem happier in a uniform of denim trousers so that you can't always tell which sex they are!

Gail was a non-stop baby – Miss Energy of 1954 even at that tender age. Eric bought an 8 mm cine camera to capture this miracle on film, and I still have 5 minutes at a time of Gail splashing in her bath. At Eric's subsequent 'film shows' everyone would say: 'Thought this was supposed to be a movie.' But you can't discourage a proud father, and if Gail blinked, Eric filmed it.

The snows melted, the sun came out and the weeks quickly passed. Work was less tiring for everyone in the pantomime once some of the matinees came off. It was a time to strike up friendships with other artistes in the show, and a certain amount of social life developed. There was the occasional party – even football matches, with the theatre taking on a local side. Stan Stennett was the top of the bill for Eric's second pantomime in Sheffield and we got to know him and his wife and young son very well. How strange that, although we didn't see a great deal of each other in all the years to come, Eric was with Stan when he died – in Stan's show.

It was shortly after this pantomime season that Eric and Ernie made their début in the medium which was to change their lives – television. And a very jolting experience it turned out to be. But first, another jolting experience.

To be on hand while doing this first television series, Eric, Gail and I had moved into yet another rented house, this time in Acton, again for a three-month period. Renting a house also made it easy for us to have our families come and visit us. But towards the end of this time we had one of our less successful ideas.

'Let's buy a caravan,' we said. 'It'll solve all our living problems,' we said. 'A home on wheels that we can tow from place to place, etc, etc.'

We had been inspired by the fact that Stan Stennett had always managed caravanning beautifully. We forgot that at one time he had driven lorries and was extremely useful as a mechanic. Why, Stan could even fly a 'plane. We could just about drive a car. Nevertheless, we bought one.

'Intrepid' being our middle name, off we drove to Manchester for a week's work in variety, the caravan hitched to the back of our Austin Hereford. We only broke a couple of cups on the way there, and collected just a wee knock on the van's nearside bodywork. The next problem was: what do you do when you arrive and there's nowhere to park? We couldn't drive round Manchester indefinitely. Finally the theatre allowed us to come to rest on a piece of waste ground near the Stage Door.

It was one of those weeks of torrential, incessant rain that I thought only happened in comic stories about Manchester. We were confined to the limited space of the caravan, with nappies piling up that couldn't be dried, until we looked like a mobile laundry. One morning I put a casserole in the calor gas cooker for our lunch. When I opened the oven door to check on the cooking, I noticed that the gas had blown out. Not thinking, I struck a match to relight it. There was a fearful explosion and I hurtled backwards. The blast was strong enough to lift Gail in her high-chair several feet but, mercifully, she was quite unhurt – just a surprised look on her face! Little flames, meanwhile, were darting about the top of my head. Help! My hair was on fire. I managed to beat them out before too much damage was done, but couldn't quite save my eyelashes. They were now little singed stubbles.

About half an hour later it hit me that there could have been a real, dreadful disaster. Suppose I hadn't opened the oven door for some while, thus allowing the gas to build up. It would certainly have been the end of 'Morecambe & Wife'. Well, not Morecambe. He was in the theatre. When he did turn up and stepped into the caravan, he didn't know whether to laugh or cry. He simply said: 'And who are you?'

When it came to caravanning, practice did not make perfect. All that business of getting it hooked on to the towing bar – and how do you get the wretched legs to stand level? Is it really supposed to list to one side? Why are the plates sliding off the table? Even the daily routine of pulling out the beds and putting them away again, plus not having hot water on tap and proper sanitary arrangements – all this might have been all right for a short holiday on a well-equipped camping site, but not for the busy life we were leading.

Apart from one beautiful summer, when Gail was getting on for two years old and we had a site near the beach at Squire's Gate, Blackpool, caravans did not work for us. Probably our worst experience was the journey we made from the North to Birchington, not far from Margate. We had broken the back of the journey without a hitch and were feeling very confident and relaxed. Then, somewhere in the vicinity of Elstree, we were confronted by a hill which, even to look at, made our hearts sink. Eric quickly changed into second gear and I clutched Gail a little tighter. Then disaster. Halfway up the hill we came to a halt and started to roll backwards, but with a caravan on tow you don't go back in a straight line. The caravan did this beautiful jack-knife across the road, and thank God there were no cars immediately behind us. However, I could see a steady stream of traffic coming up the hill; soon they would be with us. It was then that I decided to abandon ship, still with Gail in my arms, and take up traffic duty.

The other cars got the message all right – perhaps because I was

ABOVE 'Babes in the Wood' 1954–55. This babe was slightly confused at having a robber for a father! She wasn't too keen on that big black hat and cloak.
RIGHT Eric with his small daughter all dressed up in a party dress for a big occasion. The garden party was held in Blackpool and supported by all the stars from every summer show in the district. The money raised was divided between several charities.

yelling like a demented fishwife and brandishing a baby to get the point home. (Whatever became of my fashion training – elegance at all times?) In the nick of time, and red with embarrassment, Eric put the car into first gear, managed to straighten up, and off we went, feeling more than a trifle foolish. We always said that whatever we did was tinged with comedy, and it was true. So much for caravans.

To return to the TV series, the idea came from Ronnie Waldman, head of BBC-TV Light Entertainment, who developed it largely on the strength of a spot which Eric and Ernie had done for BBC-TV at the Blackpool Tower Ballroom. He was very impressed with them, and although others in the BBC still wanted to brand them as Northern comics who wouldn't succeed in the South, Ronnie was optimistic. A format for the new show was worked out. It was to be called *Running Wild*, there would be six shows, and they booked Alma Cogan as the resident singer. She was then on the verge of being a big star, and was already well known all over the country from her radio work in *Take It From Here*.

The first show went out in April 1954, at 9.40 on a Wednesday evening. Next morning the newspapers were at their throats. I do not remember, before or since, such a barrage of ugly criticism. It was almost as if there was a conspiracy to knock Morecambe and Wise on the head before they had even started. One line was typical of the others:

'Definition of the week. TV set – the box in which they buried Morecambe and Wise.'

None of the criticism was constructive. It was all a string of smart-alecky remarks, but still very hurtful, and very perplexing.

I had seen the show the night before, and to my dying day I shall never understand why the Press thought it was such a disaster. As someone who was familiar with their work, I saw there was nothing particularly original about the format of the show. At the same time, I knew that Eric and Ernie were doing as they were told and working to a script, which didn't seem at all bad to us. These were the early, experimental days of television, and they had to rely on others to guide them; but the result obviously wasn't to the critics' liking.

When Eric and Ernie did what they believed to be right for them, they seldom put a foot wrong. The only times they went astray were when they did what other people told them, because they thought: 'These are the masters. They must be right.' This applied particularly to their work in films in the Sixties, but it also has a bearing on their first TV series.

Few people knew much in those days about television comedy, because it was still so new. It was certainly hard on Eric and Ernie to be picked out for this sledgehammer treatment. In 1954 they didn't regard themselves as a big act – in the world of variety and pantomime they were still second-top rather than top-of-the-bill performers. So it was a shattering experience to be given an opportunity to try something new, to work in the medium which everyone said was 'The Future', and then be instantly rejected.

Running Wild undermined Eric and Ernie's confidence badly and they even tried to persuade Ronnie Waldman to scrap the series, but he had faith in them and asked them to stick it out. So they did, and it was probably the right decision, but by the end their morale was very low indeed. It didn't seem to be the best of times to travel up to Manchester and appear on the bill at the Ardwick Hippodrome but to their credit they took up the challenge to prove themselves again, and wondered if the audience would accept them after their TV failure. On the opening night they won a standing ovation. All was well.

Being successful in Manchester did a lot to renew their enthusiasm. They discovered that the public were on their side and delighted in their style of humour. But now they hesitated to risk a repeat of *Running Wild*. Eric's immediate reaction, whenever the prospect of television work came up, was to say he only wanted to do short spots on other people's shows. It was a long time before he felt ready to tackle something bigger, and in fact seven years went by before he and Ernie starred in their first series for ATV – the series that took them to the top.

In the summer we were back in Blackpool, on the caravan site at Squire's Gate near the sea. We were in a special enclosure for show business folk who were working in various Blackpool theatres for the summer. Blackpool was a real hub of entertainment during the summer seasons, and all the top-line performers in light entertainment would work there.

LEFT Sadie with Gail at Morecambe.
OPPOSITE TOP The caravan successfully parked at Squires Gate, Blackpool, for the summer season.
OPPOSITE BOTTOM Central Pier 1955. No prizes for guessing who the other young up-and-coming comedian on the bill was. Did someone say Ken Dodd?

The weather was marvellous, and I'd never felt fitter or been more tanned. At the end of the season we towed the caravan to Morecambe and left it in a farmer's field before going back on tour and staying in digs. It was the last time we used the van. The only other time we used a caravan was one summer in Weymouth, but that was some while later, when we had Gary, our second child, and we did it because it was impossible to rent a house in the town for love or money. Our own caravan had long since been sold and so we hired one. Ernie and Doreen were in the same predicament and they too stayed on the site.

We planned Gary, and he returned the compliment by arriving on the dot, two and a half years after Gail. By then my family had moved up to London from Margate and become tenants of the Torrington Arms, a big Victorian pub in North Finchley, and when I knew I was expecting Gary we moved in with them. Eric still had to go off on various enagements, of course, but now we needed a place of our own, which would be a permanent base – our first after more than three years of marriage.

We didn't have a lot to spend, but we had saved enough to buy a large, old, run-down, semi-detached Victorian house in a pleasant road near the Torrington Arms. I found a local builder, plans were drawn up, permission granted, and work began to convert the house into two self-contained flats, one of which we would live in and the other we would sell. We kept for ourselves the ground-floor flat: it had two bedrooms, kitchen, bathroom, spacious sitting-cum-dining room and a lovely big garden for the children to play in. We really felt we had been pretty enterprising to fix things as we had. We would soon be settled in the new flat, then I would have the baby, and everything would be fine.

Unfortunately, builders are builders, and completion dates don't always count for much. When we drew up our plans, there was time to finish all the conversion work and instal ourselves well before the baby was due. In real life, Gary was not only born, he was *crawling* before we moved in; he must have been at least six months old.

I had Gary in a nursing home in Enfield, and my very last act the previous evening was to visit our unfinished home and chivvy the builders. I went into labour at about six in the morning, but everything seemed normal, no need to panic, so I made everyone a cup of tea. Then I felt the contractions increasing, and I said to Eric:

'I don't want to alarm you, but I am going to have this baby shortly. So when you've finished your tea you'd better run me to the nursing home.'

Eric never got dressed more quickly in his life! To add to his problems – and he was more anxious than anyone – he was due to appear on television that evening. He and Ernie were guests on the Winifred Attwell Show and he would have to leave for the studio that afternoon, come what may.

For a while he stayed with me at the nursing home, willing the baby to get a move on and make an appearance. At that point I was thinking: 'What on earth do I want another baby for! I must be mad! Nothing is worth going through all this for!' I wonder how many expectant mums have had the same thoughts. So, rather than have Eric pacing the floor, I persuaded him to return home. Yes, the nursing staff assured him, someone would telephone the moment anything happened.

Not the most patient person at the best of times, Eric didn't wait for a call. He phoned in at regular intervals – too regular – and finally an exasperated nurse said: 'Mr Morecambe, there is absolutely no chance of this baby arriving before evening.'

At three o'clock, his deadline for leaving to get to the studio, he said to my mother: 'It's no good, I've got to ring just once more, no matter what they say.' He rang, and I obligingly had the baby. There was just time for Eric to make a slight detour on his way to the studio, deliver a hug and a kiss for his wife and new son, and off he went to give a much more relaxed performance than had once seemed likely.

Gary, the star of the moment, had arrived with little trouble, a perfect birth. He was a beautiful baby weighing in at $9\frac{1}{2}$ pounds, and I lay there grinning at him from ear to ear. Of course it had all been worthwhile. I ought to think about having a large family!

With the flat not ready to occupy, it was back to The Torrington for us. So there we were, Eric and I with two little ones and my brother, Alan, and his wife Pam with two also, and another due in a few months time. Before we eventually moved into our new home we had five children between us under the age of five. We could almost have started our own nursery! The eldest was their Clive, followed by our Gail, their Paul, our Gary and their Martin. We seemed to have a system worked out.

The great day came when the builders' work was finished, a lovely new carpet laid, and furniture chosen. The first item to arrive was a large television set, for us an essential piece of furniture. I still have a mental picture of Eric walking into the empty flat, pulling up the one and only chair and switching on, oblivious to all that was going on around him. He was home.

4
The Comedian's Wife

One day when Gail was very small and still our only child I took her backstage at Swansea where Eric and Ernie were appearing in pantomime. The chorus girls were very struck with her and asked if they could take her off to their dressing-room.

Nothing mischievous was intended, but for a bit of fun they made up Gail's face with powder, lipstick and rouge. She was loving every moment of all this attention, but Eric was quite cross when he saw her. He didn't want Gail to be treated like a doll, and said that no child of his was to spend a lot of time in the theatre, where she would be spoilt and develop precocious ways. He wanted a normal upbringing for his children, without any show-business frills.

We found, as time went by, that as a father Eric was in the awkward position of never being at home long enough to exert a steady influence. After a week spent performing in a theatre somewhere he would travel home to North Finchley on the Saturday night, which meant he got in very late. Next morning he would be lying in, to try and catch up on his sleep, at a time when the children were roaring around the place. By the time he was ready for them, part of the precious day-off was already gone and it would be another week before he saw them again.

There was always this conflict between show business hours and family life. When the children were young, they saw a great deal more of me than Eric, and it was really left to me to bring them up. Eric felt guilty with this arrangement, because it was more one-sided than he would have liked. He was a warm and loving dad, not over-blessed with patience but well aware of any shortcomings he may have had. Nor was he good at mechanical jobs, which he regretted because he felt that the father of a boy should always be able to assemble kits and bits of machinery and make them work – which he never could. All the same, you can't have everything. Very few men are such good all-rounders that they can be perfect at their job, a model husband and father, a mechanical genius, and always there when needed. The *main* thing that Eric did was work. Humour was his life, and he could never really get away from it. That was why, when it came to marriage and starting a family, he knew that he needed someone like me, temperamentally his opposite, who could cope when he wasn't around.

Even though my own family were only a short distance away, they were very wrapped up in their business and I found it a lonely life in the flat. I enjoyed choosing the furniture and setting up a proper home for the first time. Some of the pieces we bought in 1957 are still with us, and even the three-piece suite stayed in the family until last year.

Occasionally, Eric would bring a friend home from the show to stay the weekend. We didn't have a spare bedroom, so when we bought our suite we purposely chose one which had a bed-settee. A very comfortable bed it made, too. Even after twenty-seven years, when we let it go, that suite looked almost as good as new. (Whoever has it now will never guess they've got Eric Morecambe's old three-piece suite, or know the life it has led, slept on by an amazing cast of pantomime and variety artistes in the late 'fifties and 'sixties.)

It was really one of those grand pieces of furniture which families grow up with and which becomes part of the domestic landscape. It went through three types of covering: it started life with a very traditional look, in green damask with a gold fringe around the bottom; then it had its first amethyst phase, covered in a nylon velvet which made it look plusher and more luxurious; as it slipped into middle age, we gave it a country look with loose covers that matched the curtains. Then I passed it on to Gail for the early years of her marriage, and it went back to stage two; it spent a few years like this, a very well-preserved dowager amongst all Gail's new pieces, until one day, just before she was going to move house, she rang up and asked:

Gail was more interested in the cowboy hats in the background. She finished up having one of course.

'Mum, would you think it really dreadful if I got rid of the old three-piece suite? I won't get anything for it, but it's such a weight, we feel it's not worth transporting to our new place.'

I agreed. It certainly was a weight, with an iron base which seemed like half a ton when you tried to move it, and I could well see it had outlived its usefulness for our family, even if it did have many years of service left in it. The arms were still in excellent shape, the springing was fine – there is no doubt that 1957 was a very solid year for furniture.

Because we were very keen on having good-quality pieces in our first home, Eric and I spent what to us was a fortune on the major items, like the dining-room suite which consisted of a hand-made, Queen Anne-style walnut table and chairs, with a sideboard and wine cabinet. Gail has it to this day, and because it is such good quality it is probably worth more than we paid for it all those years ago. At the time, although Eric said that looking at the price tags made his eyes water, we were determined to buy the best we could.

Our baby grand piano is another piece that dates from 1957. My mother gave it to us, and it now stands in the sitting-room at Harpenden. Its insides have been re-done, and only recently we had it French-polished, but it is still the same piano that first came to live with us in North Finchley. The other main difference is that the top also serves as a photographic gallery, with framed pictures of family weddings, and others from show-business occasions. We have Cary Grant on our piano, the Duchess of Kent, Prince Charles, Princess Alexandra, the Queen Mother and the late Earl Mountbatten. Now, too, I keep a framed cartoon on the piano. It was drawn by Mac for the *Daily Mail* after Eric died, and it shows him skipping off-stage; the caption reads: 'You brought us sunshine, you brought us laughter, you brought us love.'

Across the road from our flat was a small park with swings and a slide, and each day I took Gail and Gary there before tea. Gail started at a nursery school nearby, and Gary was christened at the local church together with his cousin Martin. The upstairs flat was sold, and a delightful lady moved in. She was called Miss Belcher, and we never referred to her by any other name. She had worked all her life as a nanny, and her employer had bought the flat for her. To us she seemed old in 1957, but she lived in the house until very recently, when she must have been well into her nineties. At ninety-two, she had a pacemaker fitted, but she had a fall while she was in hospital, broke a hip and never really recovered from it; she died about two years later.

Living in North Finchley was my first real contact with the suburbs and we stayed for four years, but without feeling as though we had any roots there. Our social life was naturally limited by Eric's work. When he was at home, we went to the theatre as much as we could, and we'd spend some evenings with Eric's agent, Frank Pope, and his wife, who lived in Stanmore. We would go to each other's homes for supper and a game of cards.

OPPOSITE LEFT Enjoying the sun before it's time for Eric to get ready for the show at the Central Pier, Blackpool 1955. CENTRE Joan. RIGHT The Boss!
BELOW Early signs of Gail wanting to take up riding. She was under two years of age when this was taken.

We were also friendly with Terry Hall, of Lenny the Lion fame, and his wife who lived nearby and sometimes we went to the theatre with them. With show-business people it was the old problem; if you yourself were free, the others would be away working, and vice versa. It wasn't until Eric and Ernie made an impact in television that the pattern of our lives changed, with Eric switching to something like conventional business hours, working on scripts and rehearsing in the studio during the day and coming home in the evening. But all that was later.

Although the touring days of Eric and Ernie were drawing to a close, they still worked long seasons in summer shows and pantomimes. Summer seasons were a joy to the children, like having long extended holidays by the sea. We would join Eric as soon as the schools broke up, and not return until the new term was about to start. We had visits from parents, nephews and school friends. How lovely it was for us all to explore the surrounding countryside, go to the beach and visit the local places of interest. We would go off for long walks together, which was something Eric had enjoyed since he was a boy. The atmosphere was relaxed and free and easy.

We stayed at the flat in North Finchley for four years, but by the third year we began to grow a little disenchanted with living in the suburbs. We were not *in* London, amongst the interesting life, nor were we in the country, which we both loved. We decided to start looking for somewhere that would be suitable for Eric's work and give us more enjoyment as a family.

We took to exploring in the car. We would pick an area on the map and then drive to it. Apart from wanting to be on a good route for visiting parents from time to time, we had no special ties and felt free to go more or less where we wanted. In the end it was a builder doing a job in our kitchen who put us on the right track.

'Oh, yes,' he said, 'I know where I'm going when I retire. Harpenden.'

'Where?' we said. We had never heard of it. Once we realized it was really not far away, we wanted to go and see for ourselves. That same day we drove to look at Harpenden, and loved it. We loved the common land, and the golf links which give a broad open approach to the village (we still call it a village even though it is now a small town). We found it all so attractive – the wide main street with trees running along it. There and then we decided that Harpenden was the place for us. It was clear that the standard of property development around the village was high, so we contacted the main builder and bought a plot of land. A house was designed for us, and in 1961 we moved in. We lived there very happily for six years, and then moved into our present house which is larger but only about a mile away. I still walk our dog Barney round by the old house, and it gives me pleasure to see the trees which I planted and which are now enormous compared with the sticks-with-leaves they once were.

When we first went to Harpenden we were geographically in an ideal position. It was only a short run to The Torrington; there was a good train service to London, and also, the year we moved in, Eric and Ernie were just beginning to work for ATV, whose studios were at Elstree. The M1 had opened in 1959 and this and the other motorways being built were to save show-business people an awful lot of aggravation and wasted time in the future. There was the advantage of being able to get up to see Sadie and George with far less trouble, as well as having good access to theatre and club dates in Birmingham, Manchester, Leeds, Nottingham and all those other towns which had once seemed such a daunting distance away.

And what of the children? During all the time I was being kept busy as chief homemaker for the Morecambes (or Bartholomews, we have always answered to both), Gail and Gary were naturally my greatest concern and my greatest pleasure.

I accepted from an early stage that Gail, as she rushed around the often cramped living quarters in our various digs, rented houses and the dreaded caravan, bouncing off the furniture like the last shot in a pin-ball machine, was a danger to herself. The challenge of keeping her alive and well was largely successful, and in the end we came through, but we did have our anxious moments.

She was lucky to escape without injury when we had the gas blow-out in Manchester, but as I was the cause of that we needn't go into it any further!

My next heartstopper with Gail was on the caravan site at Squire's Gate, Blackpool. She wasn't yet two years old and I had taken her over to the swings; they were very crowded and so I couldn't let her go on them. I was walking away with her when suddenly, in a burst of temper, she pulled her hand out of mine and ran back towards the swings. I made a grab at her but missed. I could see all too clearly what was going to happen. An older girl on one of the swings had reached the top of her backward arc and was beginning to come flying down. There was nothing she could do to stop herself. I heard the crack as the swing seat hit Gail full on the side of the face, sending her flying backwards.

She was quite conscious when I picked her up, but she was badly hurt and shocked and I rushed her to a doctor. He patched her up as best he could, and reassured me that there should be no lasting disfigurement, and except for an enormous swelling and bruising no damage was done. How lucky we were, for it had caught Gail just beneath the eye; I thanked God it hadn't been a fraction higher.

Eric was at the theatre during all this, and Gail had settled in bed when he came in. I decided I would give him his dinner and let him relax before I broke the news, because I knew he would be terribly upset – and he was.

I tried not to let anything show in my face, but Eric somehow always knew. He had hardly sat down before he said:

'What's wrong? It's Gail, isn't it?'

Of course, I couldn't hide her, and Eric was horrified when he saw her face. For a while he wanted to blame me, but once he had vented some of his feelings and got over the shock, he calmed down.

For many weeks Gail looked as though she had gone ten rounds with Henry Cooper, and oh! those suspicious looks I would get when taking her out in public. We took care only to reveal her better side when photographs were taken and she appears in several at a garden fete with the singers Alma Cogan and Joan Regan. Eventually the swelling and bruising subsided, though for years she had a small mark on her face.

Much later on in Gail's life she went to school at St George's, Harpenden, where she was extremely happy and, though not the most academic of children, she had some passes at 'O' level. She had a flair for music and enjoyed singing in the choir. One year Gail won the school's much coveted prize for music. Best of all she liked sport; she was good at games and also became very keen on riding.

At our second house in Harpenden, where we moved in 1967, there were stables and a small paddock, and Gail was soon able to make use of them. One Sunday when she was about fifteen years old she was out riding with a friend when her horse, Melody, suddenly took fright and plunged off towards a railway bridge with Gail now clinging onto the horse's neck. She decided that her best course of action was to jump off and try to calm Melody down. Before she knew what had happened, the horse reared, and one hoof caught her full in the face.

That same day Eric had arrived home from doing an Ed Sullivan Show in New York, and he and I were chatting in the sitting-room when a car drove up with Gail inside. People from a nearby house had kindly come to her aid while her girl friend retrieved the horse. Our doctor came straightaway and he also contacted the dentist. Gail's front teeth were not only loosened but two of them were now impacted into the roof of her mouth. She also had a fractured nose and jaw, and looked a dreadful mess. Throughout it all Gail remained calm, more concerned at the upset to us than anything else.

LEFT Big sister mothering baby brother. She looked on him as being a large doll to play with. BELOW Our temporary caravan homes in Weymouth for the summer season.

It seemed an age before her face was properly healed. In Mount Vernon Hospital they tidied her up and removed the impacted teeth. All highly unpleasant, but again it could have been so much worse. I know she still rides horses!

Gary's childhood, by contrast, was not highlighted by accidents and near-disasters. But in 1958 I had to face a different kind of dilemma which affected them both.

We were staying in Morecambe whilst Eric and Ernie were appearing at a nearby theatre. I was actually in the theatre – which was unusual for me – when the telegram arrived. Eric and Ernie were being offered a six-month tour of Australia with the Winifred Attwell Show.

Everyone's first reaction was: how fantastic. Australia. The other side of the world. Marvellous.

Eric and I had no difficulty in seeing ourselves instantly transported there, to spend the warmest winter of our lives in a far-off country we would never forget. Then we remembered the children.

As far as I was concerned, I had two choices. I could either go to Australia with my husband and leave the children behind, or I could wave goodbye to Eric for six months.

As far as Eric was concerned, he was never in any doubt that he and Ernie should accept the tour. After all those years of pounding the variety circuit, they felt they deserved a change and a chance to see something of the world. It wasn't a holiday, they would have to work their passage, but they regarded the offer as a wonderful opportunity not to be missed – it might never happen again. If they had turned this chance down, they would never have forgiven themselves.

An additional bonus was that they had something in the book to come home to. It would have been professional suicide to walk off the scene and vanish for half a year. As it was, they were already booked to appear in Blackpool for the 1959 summer season, so they didn't have to worry about being 'forgotten' or having to fight for a booking when they returned.

Eric was sure in his mind, and I agreed with him, that we couldn't take the children with us. Gail would then be five and Gary only two and a half, they were simply too young. Those were the days of

Pantomime at the Hippodrome, Coventry 1957/8 'Puss in Boots'. Here we have Herbert Hare on the left with Ernie, Eric and Harry Secombe.

propeller aircraft, and the flying time to Australia was about three days – gruelling enough for adults, yet alone children. And what about when we got there? We had no idea what it would be like or whether we'd be able to find a flat to live in, or something other than hotel accommodation.

There was also the question of expense. The boys were getting quite good money for the tour, but we calculated that we would have little left over once we'd paid for all our living expenses. I came to the conclusion that I couldn't possibly go. It wouldn't be fair on the children; also, more than anything, I couldn't face the thought of not seeing them for such a long period. Why, they had never been left for even a day.

We were staying with Sadie and George at the time and it was Sadie who said quite bluntly that it would be wrong to make Eric go by himself.

'What about your marriage?' she said. 'It's just asking for trouble. Your husband should come first.'

It was also Sadie who offered the only possible solution by saying that she would be more than happy to look after the children – in fact she and George would just love to have them to themselves without us being around!

I went through it all in my mind. Gail wouldn't fret, she was due to go to school in Morecambe – the same junior school which Eric had been to – and she was very excited about that. When we put it to her that we might need to go away for a while, her attitude was quite sensible. As she saw it, Mummy and Daddy could go off and work and she would stay with Nanna and Poppa – whom she could twist around her little finger!

The one big advantage, and it just happened to work out that way, was that immediately preceding the Australian trip we would be based in Morecambe for a whole season. Both children would be nicely settled. All the same, it wouldn't be easy for Gary to be parted from us; he was only half Gail's age and still very much a baby. How would he take the sudden disappearance of his parents?

Sadie was extremely understanding. She said: 'Look, all I can do is to promise faithfully that if the children fret too much, and we feel that we can't fill the gap for you, then we'll telephone and you can catch the next 'plane back. In any case, I'll write a long letter every week telling you how they are getting on.'

I was won round, and Eric and I set off for Australia. Sadie was true to her word, and every week a long report arrived which was immensely reassuring for both of us. In actual fact it did take Gary a little while to settle, but Sadie decided all would come right sooner or later, as it did. I knew that Sadie and George thought the world of their grandchildren and they gave them all their time. The ultimate proof of this came when we returned to Morecambe and found, instead of a little plump Nanna, a slim trim Nanna who had worked off all her weight looking after the children.

Our trip to Australia was a bitter-sweet experience. On the plus side, we travelled out there via the United States, purposely taking a week over the trip. In the company of Ernie and Doreen, we made lightning tours of New York, Los Angeles and San Francisco, flew on to Honolulu, touching down briefly to refuel at Canton Island in the Pacific, and eventually landed in Sydney. Already we had seen many marvellous places for the first time. Then, as soon as we reached Australia, homesickness set in!

We could never lose this gut feeling that we had 'deserted' our children in their most crucial formative years. No matter what anyone says, six months is a very long time to be separated from your young children, and the result for us was that we just longed for the day when we could go home and be with them. We were receiving weekly reassurances from Sadie that everything at home was fine (plus little messages of love from Gail at the bottom of the page). So I stayed, and we saw out the six months together.

We received wonderful hospitality in both Melbourne and Sydney, spending three months in each city, and were amazed at the number of Lancashire people who had emigrated there, and who made a

A few of the Lancashire friends we made in Melbourne, Australia, showing us around one of the national parks.

point of coming to see us. There was even a Lancashire Society in Melbourne and we were taken under their wing. Off we would go on a Sunday, usually three or four cars in our group, and we would be shown many of the outlying interesting places: Healsville Animal Sanctuary, Maroonda Dam and many others come to mind. In Sydney we had friends and distant relatives to look up, and they too showed us the sights as well as cooking us many a lovely Sunday lunch. One trip that stood out in our minds was to the Blue Mountains.

Our funds were limited and we made them stretch as far as possible. Some of the little economies we made were quite daft – like not treating ourselves to ice creams, as if that would have made much difference. We regularly sent money back to Morecambe to help pay for the children's keep and to buy little luxuries for all of them. Sadie and George were not well off because all his life George had only brought in a basic wage as a corporation worker. Yet I never met a more contented man than George. It didn't matter how early he got up in the morning you'd know he was about from the sound of him whistling! I cannot ever remember seeing him bad-tempered.

No longer a baby. Gary looking as if he never ever got up to any mischief!

We didn't buy many souvenirs except for half a dozen lovely sheepskin rugs which we sent home as gifts for various members of the family. We certainly bought no new clothes, or not until the very end of our stay, by which time the seasons were changing and we were coming home. I needed something more than thin cotton dresses, so I went out and bought a couple of skirts and a woolly; but that was all. Later, Doreen and I reckoned that we must be the only two women to have made a six-month trip across the world and still come home not a pound overweight on our luggage!

Quite by chance we all became involved in the Test series between England and Australia. Eric and Ernie were both keen on cricket, but the game meant little to me or Doreen. Perhaps it was because our own country was playing and we were in a foreign land, but we too became amazingly hooked on the matches, never missing a day's play. We met and made friends with some of the England team and I remember them coming to our flat at Bondi Beach for a supper party. I cooked them a roast turkey – and I don't know why on earth I should remember that! We became especially friendly with Tony Lock, who later settled in Australia; the climate must have suited him because when I met him a few years ago at a function over here he was looking quite rotund. But then, we were all much younger in those days.

Earlier in this chapter I recounted a couple of the accidents suffered by Gail when she was a child. In fairness to her, I had better also describe my near-disaster at sea while I was in Australia.

We went to spend the day with Winifred Attwell and her husband at their beach house, along with Ernie and Doreen. The others were happily chatting while we waited for lunch to cook, and so I went off by myself for a quick swim. I waded into the water and swam out quite some way before I decided it was time to swim back to the beach. I hadn't realized until then just how strong the undertow was – and the tide was going out. Soon I found that the harder I swam towards the shore, the further I was pulled out to sea.

My first reaction, knowing that there were lifeguards along the beach, was to think how humiliating it would be to have to wave for help. I told myself not to panic, and kept going. But the strong pull of the currents was too much for me; I was growing more and more tired and then I got a stitch. I thought: 'Hello. This is where I either drown or get help.'

Almost as soon as I put my arm up, the lifeguards spotted me and two of them swam out with a long lifeline – standard equipment for emergencies! In no time at all they reached me and I was towed back to shore. Greatly embarrassed by the whole procedure, I thanked them and then, when I had got my breath back, walked to the

Attwell house and pretended that nothing had happened.

I kept quiet because there was no need for anyone to be concerned: the incident was over. I knew that if Eric found out, he would make a huge fuss in future every time I went in the sea. It would be: 'Don't go out too far' and 'Mind the currents' and 'Better stay in your depth' and 'Why not leave it till tomorrow?' and ...

For years I didn't breathe a word about my 'rescue', then about two years ago it slipped out in conversation with some friends. Eric's mouth dropped. He couldn't believe it. He said:

'Do you *mean* that in all these years you have never told me that you nearly drowned when we were in Australia? I thought women couldn't keep a secret.'

A charity football match during panto season at Derby. Do you recognise Eric without his glasses? Stan Stennett is in the front with his young son Roger.

I laughed and said: 'You *see*? This woman can.'

Eric couldn't get over it. It became his latest story. He told everyone about the time we were in Australia and his wife had been brought in by the lifeguards. Nobody knew about it until then – but now everybody did! He would go on, adding that it was just as well the lifeguards had been quick because there were sharks out there. She could have ended up as a shark's lunch ... This last part was probably true, but I never bothered to mention the fact to Eric.

Our journey home from Australia lasted just over a week and was an object lesson in how not to see the world. We had a three-day stopover in New Zealand, intending to see absolutely everything, but we hit torrential rain. We wanted to visit Rotorua and see the remarkable hot springs there. The four of us set out by car but the weather was so bad we had to turn back. In fact, we hardly got out of the hotel.

Then we were in Fiji for two days, amid unbearable humidity. We felt we were gasping for breath the whole time, and that was really how we spent our stay there – trying to breathe. Sleep was out of the question; we couldn't eat, and we were perpetually uncomfortable. Someone told us of a swimming pool near the airport and we drove there. What a joy this is going to be, we thought. We thought wrong. It was the only time that I've ever swum in water the temperature of bath water. It gives you the loveliest bright pink complexion – if you like that sort of thing!

We couldn't wait for our 'plane to arrive and take us away. It wasn't Fiji's fault, just a mistake on our part to have gone at that time of year and for too short a stay.

One of our last stops was Las Vegas, which was a lot of fun. Eric and Ernie wanted to see as many of the shows as they could and we would be up until the early hours of the morning cramming in as much as possible. It was thoroughly enjoyable, though we couldn't have kept the pace up for many more days. Although everything in Vegas revolves around gambling there are a lot of other attractions. First of course the shows, but also the hotels are good, with restaurants which never seem to close, swimming pools, and plenty of sunshine.

New York was our last stop and then home to England. From

Heathrow we all went to The Torrington and to me it felt as though I'd been away a lifetime; although the trip back had been a wonderful experience it was with a sense of relief that we greeted the family. There wasn't any chance of Eric and me going up to Morecambe that day, but the following morning we were off like a shot out of a gun.

There they were at the house waiting for us. The children in wonderful spirits, Sadie many pounds lighter and fitter, and George grinning happily and full of all the news that had happened whilst we'd been gone. They were going to miss having their grandchildren around after six months, but at least the summer season would soon be upon us, and we would still only be in Blackpool which is near at hand.

Eric's immediate professional future was secure, but we were very much aware that show business as we had known it was undergoing drastic changes. Theatres were closing all the time and variety bills were no longer popular. Frank Pope, the boys' agent, had nothing to offer them after the summer. It was a crisis time for him too, for he held the sole booking rights for the Butterworth chain of theatres, but that circuit was now closing.

Television was the future. It was vital to adapt to this new medium or retire early from the business. Only the performers who could make the transition would survive. Many acts not suited to television were simply fading from the scene.

Eric and Ernie came to two conclusions. Firstly, they would have to find a new agent, one with a broader range of contacts. Secondly, they would have to meet and overcome the Monster – television.

5
Chippy

Before we move on to the television years and all that followed, I should like to introduce another very influential member of the family. Many pets have paraded through the Morecambe household: horses, gerbils, cats, dogs, guinea pigs, budgerigars, fish, hamsters – creatures great and small have left their mark – but none of his successors left such a big mark as our first dog, Chippy.

I didn't want a dog at all. They did. Eric, Gail and Gary wanted a dog. I said no. How could we possibly have a dog while we were living in a caravan that was already too small for the rest of us? (This was the Weymouth caravan, which we had rented for a summer season.) It wasn't that I didn't like dogs, in fact I'd been used to having one all my life before I was married – which is how I knew the disadvantages.

I went on with my argument. When the season was over, we would be going back to North Finchley, to a flat in the suburbs of London. Yes, we did have a garden, but it really wasn't the right time or place to be saddled with all the extra responsibilities of a dog. So, no, I didn't want us to have a dog. It would be too much of a tie.

The children gave me pained looks. Eric said nothing. I could have gone on. However much the others might genuinely have wanted a dog, I knew very well that the novelty would soon wear off when it came to feeding, walking and generally taking care of a dog, and then it would be down to Mum to do it all. And I didn't want that.

Eric was crafty. He said nothing more, but a day or two later he happened to go past a pet shop ('Quite by chance,' he said later) and there in the window was a little puppy. He described it to me. It wasn't large, it looked like a Border terrier, so it wouldn't grow very big . . .

'No, Eric,' I said. 'And please don't let the children see it.'

Eric said nothing more, but a day or two later when we were all in the car together, he parked just by the pet shop. The next thing I knew, we were looking in through the window at this puppy. Eric was right. It did look like a Border terrier; it also looked extremely pathetic. As we found out later, another puppy in the litter had

ABOVE Chippy – looking as if 'butter wouldn't melt in his mouth' as a pup. No sign of the trouble he had in store for us.
LEFT Sadie with grandchild number two, Gary.

attacked it, ripped its ear and given it one or two quite nasty nips on the body. Eric hadn't mentioned any of this, but the effect on the children was terrible to my ears. As well as the usual 'Ooohs' and 'Aaahs' and 'Isn't he lovelys', there was an extra chorus of 'Oh, *poor* little thing' and 'Look at his ear, it's all torn, ooh!'

The game was all but over. Eric was about to get his own way. I went very quiet. The others went into further ecstasies. We walked into the shop, paid £6 and the puppy was ours.

We came out of the shop, went back to the car and got in. The puppy sat on the seat and looked around at us. Young as he was, he looked at his three greatest fans – at Eric, Gail and Gary – and decided there and then that he didn't want to know them. He looked at me and that was it. He sprang onto my lap, and that was how he stayed for fifteen years. He was my dog.

I was really depressed at having this dog thrust on me. He reminded me of stories about cats who always pick on people who dislike cats and won't leave them alone. I didn't know that dogs could do the same; but Chippy did. Back in the caravan, I was the only one he wanted to be with, and that included nights! Eric was quite put out by all this devotion I was receiving, while he wasn't getting a look-in. The children also felt left out. I just felt fed-up. The last thing I wanted was an untrained puppy scrabbling all over my side of the bed and trying to get his head under the sheets whenever I relaxed or dropped off to sleep.

He was a little horror. He would never take no for an answer, and in his view of the Morecambe family he was the boss, I was his soulmate, and the others came nowhere.

Back in North Finchley, we made up a bed for him in the kitchen. Eric said: 'Right. This is it. This is where he sleeps. He is *not* coming in the bedroom. He sleeps here.'

Chippy had other ideas. He began yapping and whining as soon as we shut the door. We lay in bed and listened, and could hardly believe our ears. He wouldn't stop. If he ever paused, his weariness was never more than temporary, and he soon wound himself up again to full pitch. He went on and on. How could something so small make so much noise? We were as patient as we could be. Although this awful yelping was fast getting us down, we thought he was sure to settle in the end. He didn't. At last, Eric could stand it no more.

'Right. That's it,' he said. 'I'm not having any more of this.' He got out of bed and strode into the kitchen and began lecturing the dog.

'Right!' I could hear him saying: 'I've had enough of this. Enough. It's got to stop . . .'

He didn't get any further because, as Eric stood there wagging his finger at the puppy, it bit him! Eric had to have an anti-tetanus injection in his pointing finger.

The battle went on for two or three more nights, but Chippy would not give in, and the sinking feeling began to grow in us that we were beaten. The next night we let him follow us into our bedroom.

Eric said: 'Right. I've met him halfway. He can come in here – but he is *not* getting on the bed.'

Chippy sat on the carpet and watched us. When the lights were out, I could feel his little beady eyes staring at me. As soon as we were asleep, he jumped on the bed, and stayed.

All his life Chippy never gave in. People who couldn't stand dogs admired his obstinacy and determination. Around the district, at first in North Finchley and then in Harpenden, he had a wide following of helpers and supporters. The police were especially good, because Chippy was a great wanderer and so had to be bailed out umpteen times from the police station.

Chippy hated me to leave him. If I went shopping without him, he would sit at a window and watch until I had disappeared. When I came back, he would still be in the same position; knowing him, I doubt if he had even allowed himself to blink. Then, as soon as I came through the door, he would let me have it. For about ten minutes he would bark furiously at me. His message was always the same, always very clear: 'What do you think you're doing, going out without me. How dare you!'

He was run over three times. Once by me! Sometimes he would try to get out and chase after me. I dreaded seeing him in the driving mirror, whipping round by our gatepost and hurtling after me, regardless of anything else on the road. Once he was badly hurt and had to be kept at the vet's for three months.

The vet was very fond of Chippy. He said that in his entire career Chippy was the only dog who had ever succeeded in biting him!

One year we left him with neighbours while we went on holiday for a fortnight. They insisted. We said: 'You don't want *him*. He'll be far more trouble than you think.' They said: 'No, no. Let us look after him for you. We understand him. Great little character.'

He drove them mad for two whole weeks. The only peace they had at night came when Chippy finally lost his voice.

Our summer season in Brixham was probably the happiest we ever had – even with Chippy (or Chips, as we also called him). We went for wonderful walks along the cliff-tops; the scenery was rugged and very beautiful. One day the children and I took Chippy for a walk after Eric had gone to the theatre. We followed the cliff-top path for a while, and then suddenly Chippy took off down what seemed like a sheer cliff-face, and in a matter of seconds, to my horror, he was halfway down with nothing but the sea beneath him.

We called him back, but he was enjoying himself vanishing into holes in the cliff face, probably after rabbits. After much shouting, we attracted his attention but he just stood there looking up at us. Obviously he couldn't find a way back – or so we thought.

I was wearing a pretty cotton dress of which I was very fond. I didn't want to go clambering down sharp rocks in that dress. But I had to do something or we would still be there the next day. I began, carefully and slowly, to pick my way down the cliff, thinking how foolish I was being. I edged my way carefully for a few feet, then caught my dress on a jagged rock. The material ripped and, as I disentangled myself, Chippy came flying past like a mountain goat and was back at the top before me, his little face peering down. He'd been in no difficulty at all.

It wasn't the only time I got myself into an embarrassing position with him. When we were out walking one day, he raced off into a large field which was fenced in with barbed wire and contained a herd of cattle grazing peacefully in the far corner. Chips remained oblivious to my calls, both pleading and threatening. He was an expert at 'cocking a deafun'! Finally, in exasperation, I negotiated the barbed wire and headed in the direction of Chips, who was by now interested in the activities of the cattle. The next move was totally unexpected. Cattle are by nature curious, and they began to surround Chips, who at this point took off towards me as fast as his little legs could carry him, with the cattle in pursuit. They broke from a walk into a trot, then into what seemed a stampede. Faced with this fearsome spectacle, I too turned and ran. I've since been told that the sight of a tall, long-legged woman in full flight, leaping over numerous cowpats, hotly pursued by one small dog and twenty large cows, is something that shouldn't be missed! On this occasion I didn't even tear my dress vaulting the wire fence.

Back home in Harpenden we had friends who lived in a house just a short distance away which had a view onto our rear garden. They kept a cat and were mystified for many weeks when the cat's food kept vanishing from the kitchen. Not just the food, the dish as well. Then one day Chips was spied calmly carrying the dish away and back to his own territory, where he ate the food and buried the dish in the garden. We often wondered how many plastic dishes were actually buried for posterity!

When we started going abroad for annual holidays we came round to the idea of putting Chips into kennels. We went to great pains to choose a place where he would be happy, or as happy as possible under the circumstances, and where he would be taken for walks. For many years he went to the same kennels which were run by two sisters, unmarried ladies who were devoted to dogs. We would say to him: 'Chips, you're going on your holidays to Auntie Blowers.' I'm sure he understood! The two ladies deserved a medal for 'Valour and Patience in the Face of the Enemy'. You could hear their sighs of relief when he was collected.

He carried on in the same stroppy, obstinate way for years and years. Not until he was eleven years old did he begin to show his age and a campaign grew in the family to look out for a replacement dog. The children wanted a golden retriever, and we bought a puppy – Barney, or to give him his full title 'Brambletyne Armstrong'. We were most apprehensive as to how Chips would accept this outsider, particularly a small puppy full of high spirits. Chips actually managed to completely ignore the pup for three weeks, even averting his eyes when he passed him by.

But soon he was reborn. All his aches and pains slipped away and

LEFT A cheeky look from Gail which reminds me of Eric.

BELOW Mother with her five grandchildren. Taken at the back of the old Torrington Arms before it was pulled down and rebuilt.

he couldn't wait to start all over again. When the retriever went on long walks, so did he. The arrival of Barney gave Chippy four more full years of life, and never once did he relinquish the idea that he was the boss.

I cried buckets when he died. Later I thought: why am I so upset when he had been such an absolute perisher all his days? It was true. He had been a horror to live with, quite untrainable, but everyone admired him because he was such a character – a real hundred per-center.

6
Into the Whirlpool

The man who put Eric and Ernie on the road to real success was Billy Marsh. They were upset at having to end their association with Frank Pope, and so was I because we had become personal friends. Unfortunately, this was make-or-break time and sentiment had to take second place.

Billy is one of those background figures the public seldom hears about, but he has always lived and breathed show business and is as passionately involved with it as any performer. As soon as Eric and Ernie went to see him, Billy fixed them up with a booking for the ATV show *Sunday Night at the Prince of Wales*. They shook hands on the deal, and that was the only contract they ever had. Billy handled their bookings from that moment on, all by gentleman's agreement. Perhaps it was an unusual way to do business, but none of them ever felt the need to protect their interests by signing a piece of paper. Billy then booked them a summer season in Weymouth, and by the end of the year they had appeared a dozen times in Val Parnell's *Sunday Night at the London Palladium*, six times in *Saturday Spectacular* and done four spots in *Star Time*.

It looked as though their future had been transformed, and to some extent it had. From their first meeting Billy Marsh made it clear that he could get them work – and television, their main aim, was a good possibility – as long as they could keep coming up with good, fresh material. Not for nothing was television called the Monster. It had an insatiable appetite, and was constantly calling for more. And, of course, more meant new.

What a change from the days when a music hall star could get by for the whole of his working life on a couple of good songs; if he was

LEFT An unusually 'straight' picture of Eric with the children taken at our previous home in Harpenden.
OPPOSITE 1961 in Torquay. An end of season party given by a local restaurant. Eric enjoying himself in the company of Tommy Cooper and Jimmy Jewel with his son.

a comic, he could do the same act until he retired, and hardly slip in a new joke. Television could not have been more different. It too demanded live performances, but they had to be brand-new each week.

This created enormous pressures on the performers. Scriptwriters became an essential part of the team and they too had to work under pressure. For the comedians, it wasn't simply a question of knowing the lines: no-one could be a star if they only did what was written down. They had to put their own mark on a routine, adding words, movements and bits of business. If there were musical spots in a show, these had to be devised and rehearsed with a choreographer, then the whole thing polished and gone over as many times as it took to make it not just good, but touched with a special, personal quality.

At the beginning of this new phase in their careers, Eric and Ernie were able to keep pace with the demand by working up a mixture of new material and one or two old routines which they may have tried out on the variety stage or in some earlier TV appearance, and now redeveloped. They had their judo routine, for instance, which became very popular and they were able to use it on television both here and in the United States. The sketch also contained the line 'Get out of that!' which they later used as a catchphrase.

As long as they were only being asked to do six or eight minutes, they were happy to draw on their own resources for fresh material. Their work was being well received, people were saying a lot of nice things about them, and the bookings came in steadily. Inevitably, they would graduate to having their own TV series. Television was clamouring for new talent, and their opportunity was bound to come.

When it did, it was to change their lives.

The summer after Weymouth they were in Torquay, appearing in a summer show at the newly opened Princess Theatre alongside Joan Regan, Tommy Cooper, Edmund Hockridge, and a very strong supporting cast which included a small singing group led by George Mitchell known as the George Mitchell Four. His fortunes were soon to multiply when he started his 'Singers', and so did those of virtually everyone else on the bill.

During the Torquay season Billy Marsh came on the phone to say that Leslie Grade was offering them a live thirteen-week series on ATV, starting in December. What did they think of that?

Both Eric and Ernie thought it was great and ... 'Help!' It was the opportunity they had been working towards, and the reason why they had gone to Billy Marsh. But they knew it would be a very difficult challenge to meet – thirteen live shows, or six and a half hours of comedy, to be performed in front of a studio audience and transmitted live to millions of viewers.

One thing was plain: they had to enlist the help of the best writers they could find. Ben Warriss, who was also in Torquay, recommended Sid Green and Dick Hills. Eric and Ernie agreed, because they knew that Sid and Dick had worked successfully for Jewel and Warriss, Harry Secombe, Bruce Forsyth, Roy Castle and many others. An approach was made via Billy Marsh, and in due course Sid and Dick came down to Torquay for discussions. With them they brought a tune by Johnny Mercer called *Two of a Kind*, which was to become the theme song for the shows. That meeting was the beginning of a seven-year association.

The four of them planned the first series together and it was to prove successful beyond their wildest dreams, mainly due to what at first seemed a calamity. Equity, the large show-business union, chose that moment to bring its members out on strike. This meant that suddenly the artistes were not available to work with Eric and Ernie and appear as their guests. However, it so happened that Eric and Ernie were members of a different union, the VAF (Variety Artistes Federation), so they themselves were unaffected by the strike. A format was developed with Eric and Ernie, supported by writers Sid and Dick, performing the shows almost unaided. They even took the female parts! And it worked. The shows went down very well, and by the end of the year Eric and Ernie were sufficiently popular to be invited to appear in the next Royal Command Variety Performance.

By now we were in the new house at Harpenden, and Eric was able to drive himself to work at Elstree, only twenty-five minutes away, rehearse the show and drive home for the evenings. He was free most weekends as well, so we had a much more settled home life. Instead of Eric having to dart in and out once a week like a commercial traveller, he was able to stay at home, see his children grow up, talk to me, and generally be more relaxed. We made friends locally and started to socialize – a new experience for us!

On the day of the show I would go along too, usually with a few friends. There was a great vitality and originality about Eric and Ernie's work, the audiences were wonderful, and they were able to set a pattern for many future Morecambe and Wise shows.

On those days Eric and Ernie would be working in the studio from about ten o'clock in the morning until ten at night. There were a million things to do before the public arrived in the evening, which meant going through the show repeatedly, mainly for the sake of the camera crew and studio technicians. So many little details had to be worked out and remembered such as not to step over this line, to walk from here to there and stop, to speak a line and do a quarter turn, and so on. All of which they made look so easy, as if they really did 'make it all up as they went along' – as many people seemed to think!

The ability to make material seem fresh and spontaneous is a gift I have always admired. But how do you know if what you are doing is any good? It is untried, not something which has been performed and polished on stage over a period of weeks. When it comes to television work and by the time a comic has been through his act for the twentieth time, without the benefit of any audience reaction, almost nothing seems funny. However, once Eric and Ernie were before an audience, it was magic. As Eric would say: 'Good, bad or indifferent, it's too late to worry – so let's enjoy it.' The enjoyment was contagious, and started with Eric and Ernie doing a warm-up spot of ten minutes or more to get the audience relaxed and start them laughing. Some of the material for this spot was drawn from their stage work but a great deal 'just happened' and was thought up on the spur of the moment.

Eric was marvellously quick – quick to assess the strength or weakness of anything they did and quick to add to it, or change it. Of course, he and Ernie were a perfect foil for each other. If someone forgot their lines or a prop failed, Eric could always find an ad-lib and turn a setback to their advantage. It was a great talent he had, and I cannot remember him ever being stuck for words. Sometimes an ad-lib emerged during rehearsals, and if it was good someone might say: 'Hey, that's funny. Let's keep it in.' And so the 'accident' and the ad-lib would be built into the show.

When it was over, Eric's problem was that he could never just switch off and relax. Ernie on the other hand could, for he was of a different temperament. Eric would stay on a 'high' and we would be amongst the last to leave the studio, and when we eventually arrived home it would be some time before he would go to bed. Then he would peel off his clothes, flop into bed and go out like a light. He always slept well but next morning he would be up early, as if some restless current was still running through him.

The pressures of their television schedule meant there was little time to relax before they had to go on to the next show. As one recording finished, the next would loom, waiting to be worked on, so it was continually a case of 'off with the old and on with the new', with no time to reflect on what they had just done. It was actually a very punishing routine – a show a week, written, learned and performed live, continuing at that rate until they had finished a series of thirteen shows. But, although punishing, they enjoyed those early days which proved enormously successful and satisfying. With Sid and Dick, and Colin Clews the producer, they formed an ideal team. In the whole of their career together there were really only three people who were on the same wavelength as Eric and Ernie when it came to writing comedy material, and this showed in their superb M & W scripts. Dick Hills and Sid Green were two of those people and, much later, Eddie Braben took over the role with equal success.

After their first ATV series Eric and Ernie never looked back. They had a following already, but now they began to attract that special warmth of feeling from the public which remained with them to the end. Very few stars have been able to say they were loved by the public. But Eric and Ernie were. Eric never forgot that it was the public who 'made' him, and with him the public always came first. That is why, in later years, when he was in constant demand from a variety of organizations and charities, he found it difficult to say no to their requests. I suppose we both felt that we were so lucky, had been given so much, that we must put something back into life. You can't simply take everything for granted, even if the success is all due to your own hard work, with

Proud father Harry Secombe with son David. We couldn't find the church and arrived late for the christening, to our distress. Rest of cast Jimmy Edwards, Roy Castle, Eric and Bruce Forsyth.

nothing handed out on a platter.

Most people have several sides to their nature; Eric certainly had. He could be so unrelaxed at times that you couldn't even get him to sit still long enough to have a meal. He'd be up and down like a jack-in-the-box. In his work Eric was a perfectionist and once he and television had found each other, he was hooked. It set him a new challenge and he loved it. He enjoyed the positive side too – the popularity and the rewards.

In addition to their own show, Eric and Ernie began to work in American television. Ed Sullivan saw them at the London Palladium, where they were doing a summer show with Eve Boswell, Pearl Carr and Teddy Johnston, and Bruce Forsyth, and immediately wanted them on his show. In the United States the weekly *Ed Sullivan Show* was really big, with viewing figures in the region of fifty-three million. Ed himself was one of the most successful men in the country. He travelled the world looking for new acts to bring to the American screens. For openers, Eric and Ernie were booked to do spots in three consecutive shows, and off we flew to New York.

The *Ed Sullivan Show* had a very simple format which consisted of Ed introducing one variety act after the other, with a little bit of chat before the performances. Ed, who was then about seventy, might also join in one of the routines. He loved doing this, although performing was not his strongest asset. In fact, you wondered how on earth he had ever got into show business! He was inclined to get names wrong and forget his lines, and on Eric and Ernie's first appearance he introduced them as a 'European' act called 'Morrow, Camby and Wise', which made the audience wonder why there were only two of them! He was thrilled to be included in a Morecambe and Wise number entitled *Boom Oo Yata Ta Ta*. His job was to sing the word 'Boom', and every time he saw the boys he would have a little practice.

'What was it now, boys? "Bam?" "Bom?" "Bim?"'

'No Ed. "*Boom.*"'

When they did it for real, he still got it wrong!

Ed Sullivan was very taken with Eric and Ernie, and their act went down well. Many performers were far less successful, and I can think of several top acts who were paid off before they even got to the show itself. They held an afternoon run-through which was much more of an acid test than we are used to in Britain. It was played before a carefully hand-picked studio audience who had been put together by an audience research team so that they represented the exact range and make-up of the real viewing audience. Ed would watch the run-through like an old buzzard, and he had no qualms about weeding out any act which he thought wasn't getting enough reaction from the studio audience. He went entirely on that. It didn't matter that they had travelled thousands of miles to appear on the show, or that they were a big name in the business. If they didn't click with the afternoon audience, they were out. The other off-putting thing he would do was chop and change the running order.

The Americans have always been more obsessed than us with the ratings, which were of paramount importance to the commercial firms buying advertising space. The practice over there was to put the most successful act on first, to capture the viewers and stop them switching off. Going on last – the traditional star's position in Britain – was not nearly so good in American eyes.

It was a tough school, and newcomers to the United States had to accept that their reputation at home cut no ice at all. British comedians tended to be thankful that they had been brought up on American humour, mainly through the movies, and were therefore familiar with American terms and what made them laugh. But that didn't work in reverse. American audiences were, and to a large extent still are, very isolated from other countries, and it was up to the visiting performer to prove himself, and to do it instantly.

The United States is such an enormous country, and the people are so busy with their own affairs that they have little time to look beyond their borders. Even today, I can go there and hear well-educated Americans refer to the Queen's husband as 'the King of England' – so if they haven't got used to the Duke of Edinburgh by now, I don't think they ever will!

Eric and Ernie went off to the States on a regular basis between 1964 and 1968. Sometimes I would go with them on trips, thanks to the kindness of friends living nearby who would have the children to stay, but not always. It sometimes wasn't convenient to leave the children and one occasion I was very sorry to miss was the opening

Eric with 'Charlie' – and Eric would say that he's the one with the glasses! The ventriloquist routine with 'Charlie' became a strong part of the Morecambe and Wise stage act.

of the O'Keefe Centre in Toronto. It was the Canadian equivalent of the London Palladium, and Eric and Ernie were top of the bill. I stayed at home with Gail and Gary, and Sadie and George came down from Morecambe to have a holiday with us. Unlike the time I went to Australia, school was all-important now and we could no longer go up to Morecambe during term time.

I missed Eric, and I know he missed me. However large or small the event, it is never so much fun if you are on your own, and I spent a lot of time wondering how he was managing. It would have been nice to see Niagara Falls with him, and to have been at the opening night of the show. However, the time passed quickly and I went to meet him at the airport when he arrived home. As he came through Customs, along with Ernie, Doreen and other artistes from the show and saw me waving to him, he called out in a very loud voice: 'I might as well tell you, I've had all my cameras stolen.'

And he had! They were taken out of his hotel room during his last night there, and Eric, with an early flight to catch, couldn't do much about it other than inform the police. I remember thinking, 'Damn, we've saved my fare but it's cost us the cameras!'

Eric seemed at the time to be coping with the pressures which were mounting up on him. In the three or four years since the first Morecambe and Wise series for ATV, he had become a big star on television at home and had also made his mark in the States, which was no mean feat. In addition, he had a steady stream of special performances, such as Royal Command Shows, and occasions such as show-business dinners and awards ceremonies.

Eric and Ernie were beginning to claim their own share of show-business trophies. In 1963 they were top TV Light Entertainment Personalities of the Year in the awards presented by the Guild of TV Producers and Directors, and in 1964 they won BAFTA and Variety Club awards. Clearly, in the eyes of show business they had made it; in the eyes of the public, too, they had made it. So what would happen next? How would they sustain it?

Success is such a mixed blessing. You enjoy the fruits but pay the price – and for people as highly successful and popular as they were, the demands could be daunting. A performer like Eric lived on his nerves, always concerned that he live up to people's expectations, never to disappoint, never to do an 'off' show. Physically Eric never seemed to tire, but mentally he was often shattered. He felt, acutely, not only a responsibility to himself and his family, but to managements and all those contributing to the success of Morecambe and Wise. So he would agree to most offers put to him. Besides, the money was good, so why complain. It might all end tomorrow – there was always that thought lurking at the back of his mind.

Eric had two favourite sayings: 'All of life is based on timing' and 'Comedy is based on fear'. The latter is perhaps more difficult to understand. There has never been any set recipe for making people laugh. So many times writers have tried to analyse Eric's particular gift, but Eric couldn't tell you himself and thought it a mistake even to try. Certainly, he was a 'born' comedian, a naturally funny man. But, for a professional, that isn't enough. Experience and dedication also play a great part.

Being the type of person Eric was, he took to smoking heavily. He didn't always smoke them through – he was a nervous smoker who would smoke maybe half a cigarette and stub it out, then two minutes later light up another one. I didn't give a great deal of thought to it then, because he had smoked all the time I had known him, and it was quite normal to see him with a cigarette in his hand. His Mum and Dad, too, both smoked. In the studio he was rarely without a cigarette, but it was never easy to say how many he got through in a day. Without knowing it he was living dangerously – a heavy smoker, overworking in a stressful occupation. At the time we never gave it a second thought. We took good health for granted.

Eric's work was very much his own concern – and, of course, Ernie's – and I didn't try to influence him. My main role was to provide a comfortable home background for both him and the children, and cushion Eric from other aggravations or problems which came up from time to time. My other functions included being a safety valve in times of eruptions. If he felt like letting off steam, he did. As he would say: 'I've got to be nice to people all of the time, all day long. You're the only one I can shout at!'

And what did it matter – it was all part of married life. He put me on a pedestal for thirty-two years – to him, I was in a class of my own and he never wanted anyone else. He never ceased to tell me how much he loved me, even if he shouted at me now and again!

Eric also never ceased to be grateful that I was prepared to take on the background work, which became more and more of a burden over the years. Coping with the mail, with phone calls and visitors; keeping up with the all-important diary and paperwork. As time passed I too found it a strain, but somebody had to do it; Eric already had quite enough on his plate.

Taken as a whole, the 'sixties was a decade of tremendous success for Eric and Ernie. If there was one disappointment, it concerned their movie career. In 1964 they signed to make three films for the Rank Organization, the first of which was a spy spoof called *The Intelligence*

Men. The script was by Hills and Green, and Eric and Ernie dashed along to Pinewood to begin a frantic filming session which ended three days before Boxing Day, when they were due to open in pantomime at the Palace Theatre, Manchester. The film was given a premiere in Manchester, which was all very exciting and enjoyable, but we knew as we sat watching it that this was no 'comedy classic'. It was to prove the same with the next two films, *That Riviera Touch* and *The Magnificent Two*.

Eric and Ernie wanted to bring to the screen the same originality they had brought to television, not to make films that fell into the category of being 'typical British comedies' with all the usual ingredients. For *That Riviera Touch* we had the thrill of going on location for some of the shooting in the South of France. Of course, it was mainly work for the lads – but holiday time for the wives! I don't think I have ever enjoyed a trip abroad more than that one. We stayed at the Negresco Hotel in Cannes and the beach scenes were shot in and around the area, mainly at Juan les Pins. Sometimes we were up at 5 am to travel to a location further away. It may sound anything but enjoyable, having to be up so early, but not a bit of it. The roads were empty, the weather beautiful and the scenery breathtaking. The double film crew, one English and one French, would take to the road followed by artistes, director, make-up personnel and people like myself. Not least important was the mobile canteen! You had to hand it to them, they were always first to arrive on site, and as everyone else pulled up in their vehicles they were greeted by the smell of fresh coffee and hot bread rolls. How was that for service!

We were not the only film unit staying in Cannes, and meeting up with other actors for dinner in the evening became a regular feature. Warren Mitchell spent a lot of time with us, to our mutual enjoyment, and Lionel Jeffreys too. They were filming at the time with Tony Curtis. Omar Sharif and a host of big Hollywood names were also staying at our hotel; they were in Cannes for an 'all-star' production. I didn't see anything of the making of the other two films, and once *That Riviera Touch* was finished there were no more exotic locations for us – unfortunately.

It always frustrated Eric that he never did make a really first-class film. He felt that it was the one branch of entertainment where he

hadn't succeeded, and at the back of his mind he hoped that a good script would come along with strong comedy parts for him and Ernie. Shortly before he died he saw a video of a fourth film, *Night Train to Murder* made for television, which they had just completed. Sadly, that too failed to come anywhere near his expectations.

Occasionally the Morecambe and Wise films are shown on television – and the first three look quite vintage now! In spite of their shortcomings they are enjoyed by the majority of viewers. There are some good laughs in them and they are suitable for all the family, so I imagine they will continue to be shown in the years ahead.

As the bookings began to pile up far into the future, we decided that it was essential for us to get away and have family holidays together. Just the four of us. We went to southern Spain one year and to Tenerife in the Canaries another, and in 1965 we chose the Algarve. Wherever we chose, Eric on holiday tended to attract too much attention. As soon as anyone recognized him he was looked upon as a source of entertainment, and he invariably obliged. This wasn't only with English-speaking holidaymakers. Foreign waiters were one of Eric's specialities, and from our first meal he would have them falling about laughing. The language barrier was no problem at all. From my point of view these performances livened things up if the service was slow – and kept the children entertained too.

On our first visit to Portugal we met up with Muriel Young, whom we remembered with affection from her days as a presenter on children's television programmes, later becoming a producer. Muriel and her husband owned a very pleasant villa and they introduced us to the idea of buying a plot of land which was up for sale just close by. The plans had been drawn up and a customer was being sought. At that time there was a spate of property-buying going on amongst people in our business: Cliff Richard and The Shadows had a place, and so had Frank Ifield. We were tempted, and we fell.

The Algarve was very undeveloped then, and progress, with all its mixed blessings, hadn't yet hit this land of peasants and fishermen. The tourist invasion was still to come, and in fact the Sol e Mar Hotel

OPPOSITE 'Make the most of it Sadie,' said Eric. 'This is a one off performance!'

where we stayed was about the first major hotel development in the area. The beaches were beautiful and nearly all of them deserted. It was marvellous for the children, and once we had got our villa built – which was a hair-raising experience in itself, with the added drama of a builder absconding halfway through with his advance payment – we had some wonderful holidays there. To fit in with school holidays and Eric's availability, we would go either at Easter or the beginning of September; the summer temperatures were in any case too hot for us, particularly for Eric who preferred the sixties and low seventies.

Pleasant though the villa is, and we have it still, my feelings towards it have always been mixed. If we had our time over again, I don't think I'd want any property abroad. For one thing, we never used the villa enough. If we'd been able to go there for a couple of months each year, then it would have been worthwhile, but we never had that much freedom because Eric's work, instead of decreasing as time went by, became more and more demanding.

In the 1960s the plusses were that Gail and Gary loved going there for their holidays and were able to take friends, and for Eric it was always relaxing. Often he would sit outside writing down ideas for television – work again, but he enjoyed it – and he also loved to read and listen to music.

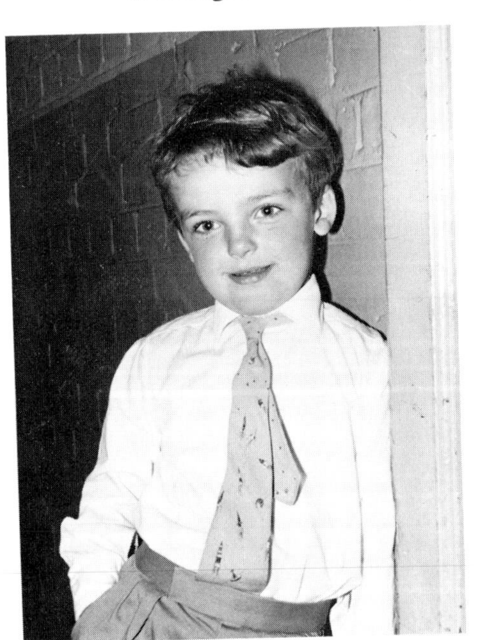

Man about town! Gary growing up.

Once we were home from holiday, it was back to the treadmill. Eric and Ernie broke records with their stage shows, including a wonderful summer show in Great Yarmouth which beat all previous theatre records. They made an LP entitled *An Evening with Ernie Wise at Eric Morecambe's Place*. Then in summer 1968 they left ATV and signed to make a new series in colour for BBC 2. They seemed to be in demand from all quarters, and had to choose between doing a West End show or a tour of Northern clubs. They opted to go north. In October 1968 they were appearing at a club in Darwen, Lancashire. They were scheduled to do a television appearance in the States, plus a new series at home, and they also had to do an eight-week theatre season in Glasgow starting at Christmas. They had recently turned down a request from Bernard Delfont to do four spots in a Royal Command Performance Show – not because they didn't appreciate the honour, but because they felt it wasn't humanly possible. They would never settle for giving less than a first-class performance with material that would do them proper justice, but the schedule was going mad. Bernard Delfont persisted about the Royal Command, and sent them a personal telegram. They gave in and accepted, but for the first time I really felt Eric's anxiety and knew that he was petrified that he wouldn't be able to cope. Perhaps it was now that he came to the conclusion that 'comedy is based on fear'.

On Sunday 3 November they opened at the famous Batley Variety Club, with an act lasting an hour and a quarter starting at midnight. It was only for two weeks and each evening Eric phoned me. He never really enjoyed club work with its late hours and atmosphere very different from the theatre which he preferred. But Batley was a good club, and he was staying at a very comfortable hotel, so when he kissed me goodbye at the beginning of the week he was quite happy and left home seemingly fit and well.

In the early hours of Friday 8 November I was woken from a deep sleep by the telephone ringing. An unknown voice said:

'Mrs Morecambe?'

'Yes.'

'Mrs Morecambe, there is nothing for you to be alarmed about, but your husband has admitted himself into hospital.'

7
Early One Morning

At first I thought it must be some kind of cruel practical joke. 'Admitted himself into hospital?' It was such an odd thing to say; I couldn't understand it. I had recently said goodbye to a perfectly fit husband, and spoken to him on the phone the previous evening. So why had he 'admitted himself' to hospital?

The voice gave me a telephone number, and suggested I rang back in an hour, when they should have more news. I rang back immediately, to check that I really had been speaking to Leeds Royal Infirmary, and that they did have Eric Morecambe. They confirmed it. An hour later I rang back and learned that he had been given a preliminary examination, and it seemed likely that he had had a heart attack. Now they were waiting for a specialist to finish examining him. As soon as they had any more news, they would ring me ... but it would be a good idea if I got myself ready to come up to Leeds.

Come up to Leeds? In my shock and bewilderment I thought: I can't go up to Leeds, not in the middle of the night, leaving Gail in bed. I was still unable to take in the bad news; not wanting to believe it was true, I hadn't yet switched into the frame of mind which deals with emergencies. I did, however, ring my brother Alan, and he said he would come over straight away and drive me up to Leeds if necessary.

Gail was then fifteen and quite able to look after herself for a few hours. I woke her up and told her the news. Mr Bedwell, our gardener, would be coming in later, and a friend would see Gail off to school. I rang Gary's boarding school and arranged for the news to be broken to him there. My brother arrived, I put some overnight things in a suitcase and eventually we were ready to leave. One way and another, several hours had passed since the first telephone call, so I rang the Infirmary before we set out to tell them I was just leaving. The voice at the other end of the line said:

'Well, you'd better hurry, or you may be too late.'

It threw me completely. My stomach turned over. Until that moment I hadn't even considered that he might die. He was forty-two years old, he had looked perfectly fit only days earlier – how could he possibly become so ill in such a short time? It seemed like a nightmare. As for the heart attack, that was beyond my understanding. People then didn't have heart attacks with the frequency they do now – at least, you didn't hear about them. I didn't know anyone who had had a heart attack. I sat in the car with Alan and didn't utter a word all the way to Leeds. Since the first phone call I felt I'd aged ten years, and the journey seemed never-ending.

By the time we arrived, I was in a dreadful state of mind. I can remember being taken into a room, and there was Eric in an oxygen tent. We looked at each other through the plastic sheeting and Eric, seeing my distress, called out:

'I'm going to be all right, you know, love. I'm not going to die.'

Never have I been so relieved to hear someone speak, and I thought immediately that he would be all right. It wasn't advisable to stay with him for long and the doctor was waiting to talk to me privately. He warned me that although Eric had been told he had had a slight heart attack, in reality it was a massive one and the next forty-eight hours would be crucial. If he could live through that period he would probably recover, but it was touch and go.

I booked into a hotel, and waited. The public interest in Eric's heart attack was enormous. The hospital was deluged with telegrams, sacks of letters, flowers, and all kinds of presents including several holy medals. Friends and journalists rang in the whole time and put the hospital switchboard under a huge strain, all of which the people at the Infirmary bore with wonderful patience and good humour.

Eric, meanwhile, pulled through the vital forty-eight hours and began to feel a little better. He was still very weak and had to be kept as quiet as possible, and this meant barring all visitors except me. He only had to see a visitor, and his electrocardiograph started bouncing all over the place. While he was in hospital, I heard the story of the night of his attack. This has been told many times, and nobody can tell it like Eric did! However . . .

His problems began with pains in his right arm which felt like rheumatism. On the Thursday night, when he and Ernie finished the show, Eric explained that he didn't feel well so would Ernie mind doing the autographs while he went back to his hotel. This signing session was a regular feature of their theatre and club work, and usually Eric was more than willing to talk to some of the audience afterwards and sign any autographs. This night he left the club, got in his car and drove off towards his hotel which was at Selby, on the other side of Leeds.

On the road he began to feel severe pains across his chest, and by the time he reached the outskirts of Leeds he knew he needed medical help. A quarter to two in the morning is not the best time to seek help in a strange town. The streets were deserted. Then along came Walter Butterworth.

Walter had been out late when Eric drove up and in a whisper asked for directions to the nearest hospital. He was by now sweating profusely and had almost lost the ability to move his arms. Then he said:

'Look, I don't feel very well. Could you possibly drive me there?'

It turned out that Walter had only ever driven tanks in the Territorials, nothing like a Jensen Interceptor, but Eric told him how easy it was with the automatic gears, and he got in.

They found one hospital which turned them away because they didn't take emergencies, and they set off to look for the Infirmary. Walter parked at the bottom of the hill leading to the hospital and went to find a wheelchair. He arrived at the wrong entrance and was directed towards Casualty. Eric, meanwhile, was feeling desperate and decided he couldn't sit around any longer. Bent double, he struggled up the hill, went to the wrong entrance also, and at long last found Walter talking to a man in a blue uniform.

Casualty was busy with the usual assortment of cut heads and bleeding noses when Eric staggered up to the man in uniform. The usual formalities had to be gone through, of course, come what may.

'Name?' said the man.

'Eric Morecambe,' came the reply – Eric was still quick enough to decide he stood more chance with that name than his real one.

'You were right,' said the man, turning to Walter, 'it is him.'

The interview proceeded until at last, with address, occupation and age given, and the facts noted that yes, he didn't feel well and wanted to be admitted, and could he please lie down, the hospital was ready

The brighter side of being in hospital. Helping Eric open up all his get well cards and letters after his heart attack in Leeds.

to receive him. Soon Eric was stretched out on a trolley. With his immediate worries taken care of, and being Eric, he began worrying about his Jensen! Any minute it could be towed away! At that moment a very young doctor arrived to take over, and in seconds Eric was being given an injection. He quickly explained about the car, and the doctor volunteered to move it. He went away for a few minutes and then returned to say that it was now safely in the car park. The keys were tossed onto Eric's chest and soon he was being sped along the corridor to the X-ray department, and another injection. The last thing he remembered was Walter's concerned face looking down and saying:

'Look, my mates will never believe me when I tell them about this. BEFORE YOU GO, could you sign this?'

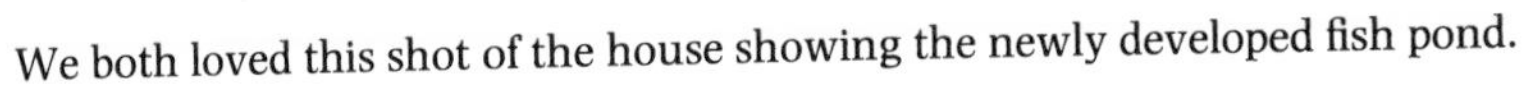

We both loved this shot of the house showing the newly developed fish pond.

He put a piece of paper on Eric's chest and Eric scrawled 'Eric Morecambe', convinced it was his last autograph!

Two weeks later a car arrived to take Eric and me home. During that time I had dashed south several times to see the children and attend to the house. A neighbour who had business commitments in Leeds had given me many a lift in his car, which proved a great blessing. Now it was time for Eric to return home. It wasn't until he tried to get out of bed and dress himself that his confidence left him. How you feel lying in bed doing nothing is very different from how you feel when the effort has to be made to stand on your own two feet. Eric had been keen to leave hospital and return home, but when the moment came he really felt that perhaps it was too soon, and so it was some time before we were actually ready and made our way carefully to the car.

The house in Harpenden (where I still live) is nice and roomy and we were able to convert the TV room into a bedsitter so that Eric didn't have to go upstairs. Gradually he began to recover his strength, but for a long time he felt extremely vulnerable, and after any exertion thought he was going to have another attack. I persuaded him one day to try walking upstairs, and he surprised himself by reaching the landing with no real trouble. He started to go for short walks, and began to take an interest in birdwatching to make the walks more interesting.

Eventually the time came when he needed some more active kind of exercise, but his own inclination was to hang about the house, where he felt safe, and not take unnecessary chances. The situation was resolved one day by our GP, Dr Price, who appeared on the doorstep and threw his car keys to Eric.

'Here,' he said, 'you need some exercise, so we're going to the golf driving range at Watford. You can take me in my car.'

Eric, who thought he had been lucky not to have a heart attack when he caught the keys, said: 'What? Me? I'm not ready for that.'

'Oh yes you are,' said the doctor. 'It's just what you need.'

They drove off, and when Eric returned he was a changed man. The outing to the driving range not only took him out of himself, it made him realize that he was capable of getting back to his normal life and show business too – if you can call that normal!

8
Life After Television

The ever-present fear for people in show business is that one day – tomorrow? – it will all come to an end. This particularly applies to those who have enjoyed the sweet smell of success. There is so much to lose, and having once reached the top, there is only one way left to go! I have heard Eric and Harry Secombe joking with each other, saying: 'We've got to give it all back tomorrow, you know!' It was said in fun, but there was that little thread of truth in it, for success doesn't necessarily last forever.

Eric and Ernie went to the top in 1961, and stayed there. Their prolonged success seems almost incredible, because there were many times when it seemed they would be unable to continue. Eric's first heart attack was a bolt from the blue and we learned to live with it, though it was a long, long time before the anxiety lurking at the back of our minds subsided. If Eric was so much as an hour late getting home, I found myself fidgeting and looking at the clock. In fact, for a long time after his illness, he would make a point of phoning if he was going to be late.

Although he made a swift recovery and was back at work in May 1969 – to everyone's surprise – we still went through a period when no money came in. This loss of earnings was not an immediate worry but it served as a warning sign that yes, indeed, it *could* all end tomorrow. We realized we should be investing for the future in other ways, both as a form of insurance against sudden or early retirement or so that if, as we hoped, Eric continued to work until the time came to wind down and retire, we would have the means to enjoy it.

The trouble was that during the Sixties taxation was running at a very high level. This is particularly hard on performers who, when their career is over, have nothing to sell. No shop, factory, small business of any sort. When he is no longer able to sell himself, there is nothing left.

We had always believed in pension schemes and insurance policies, and a few years previously, in 1964, we formed a partnership with my brother Alan and went into the hotel trade, buying the Tudor at Fenstanton, Huntingdonshire (now Cambridgeshire) and later the Golden Lion at St Ives, in the same county.

Eric was always too busy to take an active interest in the hotels, and in any case it wasn't his scene, but he went there from time to time, and in the last few years there was the extra incentive of going to see our married children. Gail is settled nearby with her husband Paul and their two children, and for a while Gary and his wife Tracey had a lovely thatched cottage in the area.

The year 1969 was also the time when Eric got to grips with his hobbies. He could never sit around doing nothing, and to help him recuperate he took up birdwatching, as I have mentioned, and renewed his interest in photography. In the course of time he developed many other passions, reaching a stage where he would say: 'My hobby is ... hobbies.' What he liked most of all was to dip into something, follow it fairly intensively for a while and then, if his enthusiasm faded, go on to something else. Some of his hobbies were related to each other, such as birdwatching and photography. He liked to study the wildlife in our garden – the birds, squirrels, pond fish and, if he was up early enough, the herons that came to visit. He was an exceptionally observant man, and keen-eyed despite his glasses. He never missed a thing.

With his fondness for birds, wherever we went he took a field guide with him, or bought one if we were abroad. If he saw a new bird, he would tick it off in the book. He never forgave me for seeing a Golden Oriole in Portugal without him – I only wished it had been him and not me!

Quite early on he lent his name to various RSPB schemes and this is something that I continue on his behalf. Their most recent venture is the sanctuary at Old Hall Marshes on the Blackwater estuary in Essex. The RSPB have bought more than 1,100 acres and opened up a grassland site next to the river where Brent Geese – about 100,000

Barney and Chippy obliging us with a simple trick, aided by half a pound of biscuits.

of them – can come and spend the winter. They are installing hides for their members and enthusiasts, and I am certain that Eric would have loved it. He would have stayed for hours with his binoculars, just watching the birds come and go, taking photographs and enjoying the whole spectacle of the countryside.

At the time of his death Eric was entering another phase of enthusiasm for photography. He had been very keen during the early years of our marriage and then put it aside, only dabbling in it if we went abroad. In spring 1984 he was raring to go again, and had overhauled all his cameras and equipment. He was also thoroughly enjoying trying to organize the family collection of hundreds and hundreds of prints, which he was putting into albums. One day I found him poring over a small mountain range of wallets and prints. He looked up and said:

'It's *amazing* how much we have done in our lives. Look at all these. However did we do so much?'

He was right. The photographs are a lasting reminder of all the places we have been to, events we have attended and people we have met. Without them there would be nothing to look back on; no permanent record. It was staggering how much we had forgotten, and then seeing a photograph it would all come flooding back: 'Good heavens, that's so-and-so and that was taken at such-and-such.'

Eric kept saying: 'You'll be surprised when you look through these albums after I've finished them ... You won't remember half of it.'

Photographs remind me not only of people and events, they link together to make a whole mosaic of one's life. Now I tell my daughter Gail to make sure she takes plenty of photographs, especially of her children. If they let their children grow up without taking photographs, in the end they will have no record of their life together. Only memories – and memories become clouded and let you down.

Eric was in no sense a gardener, but he got enormous pleasure from our garden. He once had a go at watering some flowers with my trusty old watering can. It came apart in his hands, soaking his trousers. Why should it choose that particular moment to disintegrate? We never could tell, but it was true that the actual mechanics of gardening interested Eric about as much as mending a fuse. What attracted him much more was the wildlife that made its home in and around our garden.

First, the birds. They have always been made especially welcome. We have a covered bird-table and bird-feeders and we put out nuts and scraps all through the winter – even whole loaves when the snow is down. The only trouble with having all this bird food near the house is that it attracts the squirrels, and I've never been keen to attract a squirrel indoors. From what I hear, once a squirrel gets inside a house, often squeezing itself into the attic, it can cause enormous damage. So, although I've done nothing yet, I may move the feeders and the bird-table further down the garden and watch the birds and the squirrels do battle from a distance.

Over by the fish pond we played host to a more dramatic battle between the fish and various marauding herons. Eric has always been keen on fish and fishing, his biggest hobby. When we moved to our present house there was just a small goldfish pond. We had a larger one dug out, complete with waterfall and fountain, and Eric became very enthusiastic about raising fish in it. He would buy young fish and bring them on to maturity. Some of his carp reached a huge size and were worth a good deal of money – but try telling that to a heron.

Once the first heron found Eric's fish, their future was distinctly limited. As battles go, it was a one-sided affair, because a hungry heron can easily spot his prey from the air long before the fish see him. Large carp would disappear overnight, including Eric's favourite, a monster he called Jaws which survived an extremely hard winter only to vanish suddenly in the spring. The herons didn't always carry off the fish; sometimes they would peck at them in the pond and leave them there, too damaged to recover; or we might find a dropped fish on the lawn. To defend our fish, we bought a large net and draped it over the pond, but it was so unsightly it spoiled the whole look. We kept it there for a long time but eventually decided to risk taking it off. Back came the herons, or so we presumed, because soon after that we lost a number of fish all at once. It made us wonder if some human fish-lover hadn't heard about our pond and decided to help himself. We never got to the bottom of that mystery; maybe it was a pair of herons working overtime, we shall never know.

It was always sad to lose a special fish, particularly if it had been with us for some while and we had got to know it. It was a shock to go to the pond and find the remains of what until recently had been a beautiful carp; and just as bad to find that a favourite had 'gone missing'.

Eric, as you can perhaps imagine, was a neutral observer. He loved the herons too, and would never have done anything to harm them. He just wished they wouldn't keep touching down in our garden for a tasty breakfast.

After we lost several fish in one go, a newspaper wrote a piece about it and we had letters from several very kind people suggesting various remedies. One of these was to deter other herons by putting an artificial heron next to the pond. We looked around the gardening shops and nurseries, but no-one had an ornamental heron. There were plenty of stone cherubs, or sundials, or other birds, but herons were out of fashion and we drew a blank. Until it was smashed, we used to have a stone cormorant, which isn't so very different from a heron, but now we couldn't find one of those either. We let the idea drop.

Maybe two years went by, then one day I was with Gail at a nursery near Cambridge, and found myself looking at a plastic heron, made in Italy. 'Marvellous!' I thought, so I bought it and drove it home. Eric was delighted. We placed the plastic heron beside the pond and left it there. It looked very realistic. However, we didn't honestly think it would make much difference. In any case, we hadn't seen a real heron for more than a year. Two mornings later – as close as that – I drew back the curtains in our bedroom and looked out. There, standing next to the plastic heron, was a real one!

I thought I was getting double vision! The real heron stood stock still, with its head turned slightly towards its artificial friend, until a noise disturbed it and it lifted itself into the air and flapped away. Next day it was back, disproving all known theories about artificial herons scaring off real ones. This real one thought it had found a mate! Eric said:

'If that heron tries to get off with ours, it's got a nasty shock coming!'

Fishing was Eric's chief hobby. He fished, off and on, all his life, beginning on Morecambe beach with his dad, George, who showed him how to put up what they called 'trot lines' – a series of lines suspended between poles – to catch codling, cod, flukes, plaice and anything else that came along. He learnt how to look for cockles in the sand, and sometimes they went out in a boat with some of George's friends. They also went pole-fishing on the pier, using rods made from saplings which George would find and smooth down, and drill holes to take the line.

Before he went seriously into show business at the age of fourteen, fishing was probably what Eric liked to do most of all in his free time. One of his last projects before he died was to complete a book about his fishing experiences, called *Eric Morecambe on Fishing,** which became a best-seller. (If you haven't read it, that's a plug!) I don't propose to go over the same ground in this book, partly because it has been covered already and also because, with Eric, fishing was something he liked to do by himself. I was not directly involved in his expeditions, though I always encouraged him to go, especially in the last few years of his life when he became really keen and was lucky enough to be able to fly-fish for trout on the River Test in Hampshire. His days on the Test were wonderfully enjoyable for him, and he would return home a contented and relaxed man.

Although it's a long drive from Harpenden, he could just about do it in a day if he set off early in the morning and didn't mind driving back at night. The thing about trout fishing is that early evening to dusk when the trout come up to feed is often the best time to fish and sometimes Eric would stay overnight with our friends who owned that stretch of river, or with Dickie Davies and his wife Liz, who lived nearby. Occasionally he fished with Johnny Ammonds, his producer, or with Philip Jones from Thames Television. At other times he would go out locally with Gordon Beningfield, the natural history artist who was a good friend.

Where I came into the act was on Eric's return in the evening. I could tell if he'd had a good day on the river by the way he came through the door. If it was really late, he poked his head round first, and said something apologetic like: 'Can I come in?' then I knew he'd done well and was hiding four or five trout behind his back. It's best if the fish can be gutted and frozen the same day, you see, and that was my job. Of course, if it was that late I could always pop them in the fridge until the morning – if there was room! Eric's trout season ran from May until September, and if he had several runs down to the Test fairly close to each other, the freezer would be bulging with

*Pelham Books, 1984.

The end of a perfect day.

trout. Sometimes it was so full I couldn't find anything else!

Eric's fishing was a great non-profit-making family business. He caught them, I gutted them and wrapped them in tin foil for freezing – but neither of us ate them! We could only give them away to friends. Eric never ate trout or salmon. He enjoyed white fish like cod, plaice, hake and halibut, but what he adored most was shellfish – cockles and mussels and, best of all, Morecambe Bay shrimps.

At the beginning of his health problems, he didn't have to worry about his diet, but then cholesterol became an issue and he had to be strict with himself and cut down on certain foods. He could apply great self-discipline to giving up all types of food – except for nice fresh Morecambe Bay shrimps! You wouldn't think that those tiny shrimps could contain a significant amount of cholesterol, or a significant amount of anything else, but apparently they do and so Eric had to be careful.

In 1969 he also began his famous association with Luton Town. This came about when he decided to take Gary, then aged thirteen, to his first football match. The nearest League clubs were Watford and Luton, and they were going to toss a coin to decide between them when they found that Watford were playing away that weekend. Eric rang up Luton Town FC and asked if he could bring his son along to the next match. The club said fine.

Luton were by no means a fashionable club but in a modest way they were on the way up, with a new and enterprising chairman, Tony Hunt. In 1969–70 they won promotion from the Third Division; in 1970 Eric became a director and in 1974 the club reached Division One.

Eric was not the businessman type and the boardroom side of things never exactly filled him with enthusiasm, but he did a tremendous amount for Luton Town, so much so that it is fair to say that he put them on the map and got them talked about. He was probably the only man on earth who could have fixed it to have Glenda Jackson parade on television with a banner reading 'Luton Town FC', and that banner was seen by about twenty million viewers. He raised money for the club and did many personal appearances to help them. He went to as many matches as he could – even the away games while he was a director – and of course the people from the opposition clubs were always delighted to meet him in the hospitality room at Luton when Eric, as ever, would be his friendly, humorous self, chatting to everyone and trying to make their visit a memorable one.

He enjoyed his time on the board at Luton, but I think he was relieved to give it up eventually. Football, which he always loved, was becoming secondary to working for the club, which he willingly did, but the whole idea originally was for football to be a relaxation

A spot of bribery from Eric had Melody performing for the cameraman.

and something he could go to with Gary. In 1977 he resigned as a director and became a vice-president. This absolved him from all the boardroom meetings and the political and financial worries, but still entitled him to two seats in the directors' box so that was a good outcome all round. The club could still reap the benefit of having Eric's face around at matches, and the constant plugs he gave them on TV, and for his part he was able to watch good football in comfort which was all he had ever wanted to do in the first place.

Our villa in Portugal was a very useful bolt-hole during the Seventies. While we were there one year, Eric began collecting attractive coloured pebbles from the beach. Another hobby, I thought! Then he went off and bought one of those machines for polishing the pebbles and making them into jewellery. That was one of his shorter-lived hobbies. He wouldn't let anyone help, and I'm not at all sure how far he got with his pebble-polishing, but soon enough it was put away and never seen again. As far as I know, it's still tucked away in the attic at home. Telescopes and archery equipment, in their time, had also been relegated to the attic, then later were given away.

Eric always loved gadgets and novelties. One day he was on one of his walkabouts in Harpenden when he ended up in the local art shop. There he came across an outfit for making plaster-cast chessmen from moulds. He bought it, came home with a box under his arm, but wouldn't tell anyone what was inside. Until he produced the finished chessmen we didn't know what he was up to! I think he got more fun out of coming home with a mysterious box than with the actual contents. While he was recuperating he had a phase with *Scalextric* cars which he laid out on the sitting-room floor. We bought him an indoor putting set which he quite enjoyed. For a short time both broke the monotony of convalescing.

The idea of Celebrity golf matches really took off in the 'seventies, since when the Variety Club Golf Society has collected masses of money for charity by staging tournaments such as the Harry Secombe Classic. Usually the celebrities are sportsmen and well known people in show business. The idea caught on so well that at one time it seemed to us as though Eric was the only comedian who didn't play golf.

In fact, he did like golf and he and Ernie had played quite a lot back in their touring days. In the afternoons the choice was usually between golf and the cinema – which is also how they both became great film buffs! Other artistes like Arthur Askey, Bruce Forsyth, Jimmy Tarbuck and Val Doonican were very keen and went on to become superb players. When we moved to Harpenden, Eric and I joined Harpenden Golf Club and for a short while he played on the course which runs beside the back of our garden. Then he stopped, as though he had rather fallen out with the game.

If I analyse it, Eric liked playing sports for fun but he was strictly non-competitive. He never liked playing a game which required him to take it too seriously and where it was thought important to win. That was why trout fishing suited him so well: he could do it by himself with no hassle and take all the time he wanted – but, again, if he was asked to take part in a fishing competition, he would say no, except to the occasional charity event.

Strangely enough, not long before he died he said: 'I think I'm going to take up golf again.'

I couldn't believe my ears. I said: 'You're kidding! We've been paying subscriptions at the club for donkey's years, we've only just let our membership lapse, and now you want to take it up again! You can't mean it.'

'Yes,' he said, 'I think the time has come to go back to it.'

He never did.

9
Busy Days and Gala Nights

In a profile of Eric which he wrote in 1973 for the *Observer Magazine*, Kenneth Tynan traced the development of Eric and Ernie through three Marks, like a car. Mark I was the original model, a traditional male double act with Ernie the classic stooge and Eric the comic. Mark II came about in the 1960s, when they 'were no longer comic and stooge, but two egoists in more or less equal competition'. Now Ernie would get things wrong as well. This was the act which emerged from the sequence of television series that began in 1961, with Sid Green and Dick Hills writing the scripts.

Then came Mark III, which Kenneth Tynan obviously thought was their best yet. 'Eric in particular,' he wrote, 'has burgeoned into one of the most richly quirkish and hypnotic performers in the history of the box.'

This was the character fashioned by Eric from scripts by Eddie Braben, who worked for them from 1969 until Eric's death. The strange thing is, Eddie might never have entered their lives at all had it not been for Eric's heart attack, which forced him to lay off work for six months. While he was recuperating, the news came through that Sid and Dick had suddenly gone to work in America and would not be available to do any more work for Eric and Ernie.

It seems that this opportunity to broaden their scope came up rather unexpectedly, and Sid and Dick simply said yes without further ado. They agreed with their agent and with Billy Marsh that they should be the ones to break the news to Eric and Ernie, but, as can happen when an unpleasant task needs doing, the moment was put off and put off until it was too late, whereupon Sid and Dick 'escaped' to America, and Eric and Ernie were left to pick up the news from an airline steward who'd seen it in his newspaper.

Once it was out in the open, Eric and Ernie always stated publicly that no one was to blame, it was simply unfortunate, and so on. But I am sure the incident left a nasty taste with Eric, who felt he'd been 'written off' by his friends Sid and Dick. All the same, the milk was spilt and it was no use crying over it. How were they going to find a new script-writer?

Eric and Ernie were having discussions about their TV work with Bill Cotton, who was Head of BBC Light Entertainment, and he came up with the name of Eddie Braben. Eddie had been writing for Ken Dodd for a long while, but now was free. He came down from Liverpool for a meeting and a new partnership was formed.

Eddie at first was doubtful, saying that he was a joke writer and couldn't do sketches or situation comedy. But the boys thought he had an original mind and asked him to write them a show. Eddie left the meeting with a few notes on a piece of paper, retired to his workroom in Liverpool and produced a full-length script which Eric and Ernie were able to use as the basis of the first of their new shows. Eddie was never keen on coming down to London, he preferred to work in solitary state from home, planning and writing an entire show which he then posted down to London. Eric and Ernie took the scripts and changed and embellished them as they saw fit, adding their own bits of business and listening also to the suggestions of Johnny Ammonds, their producer.

This was very different from the old Hills and Green method, where they met together and sketches were worked up from a single sheet of notes, but the important thing was that Eddie, from the beginning, made a big contribution to the development of Morecambe and Wise 'Mark III'. After the first trial show he wrote three more 'on approval', and then became the official script-writer for the television shows. The 'plays wot Ernie wrote' were Eddie's idea, and from that concept a lot of other things flowed, including the guest stars, the longer sketches, and the gradual transformation of Eric into a harder figure, a kind of straight man who was funny, as opposed to Ernie who became cast as the comic who tried to be funny but wasn't. As Kenneth Tynan continued:

'The combination is brilliant, wholly original, and irresistible. How much of it is due to Braben, and how much to the performers, is hard to determine; but we know that the scripts are heavily modified in rehearsal, and that most of the changes come from Eric.'

The other big difference was that while Eric and Ernie put just as much effort into their work, they actually worked less often. Once they had cleared off the remaining four half-hour shows in the series which had been interrupted by Eric's heart attack, they signed a new contract which had a lot more time built into it. The next series consisted of thirteen forty-five-minute shows but now, instead of having to complete them at the rate of one a week, they were allowed three weeks in rehearsal and two days for filming in the studio. This was an enormous improvement because it gave them the vital breathing-space they both desperately needed.

As they slipped back into harness all their old confidence returned, and soon they were making shows which everyone agreed were better than ever. For a while they were content not to take on any other commitments outside their television work, and to pace themselves in a much more realistic way. In 1968 they had very nearly let themselves be dragged under by a whirlpool of commitments. Now they said: 'We have obligations to ourselves as well, and to our families, so there's no way we're going to fall back into that state of mind which says yes each time the phone rings.'

Their workload, however, did steadily increase and 1970 found them doing Sunday concerts throughout the summer at seaside resorts. They both felt this was important because it kept them in touch with live audiences. They later increased the number of live engagements, doing two or three nights at each town. It was also extremely lucrative, and Eric began to joke about these appearances, referring to them as 'bank raids'. Life was now busy but, even so, Eric found time to be at home, to take up his hobbies (as we have seen) and also to switch off and enjoy his own company.

When he was with people, whatever the occasion, he had a compulsion to be entertaining. It was simply the way he was made. He couldn't have been any different, and if ever he did try to relax and keep a low profile, people would start worrying and thinking he didn't feel well! And so he had the reputation of being marvellous

ABOVE Only once a year are ladies invited to the Long Room at Lord's to a party given by the Lord's Taverners. Here we are with Judith Chalmers and Arthur Askey.
LEFT Eric receiving his Doctorate at Lancaster University from their Chancellor, Princess Alexandra.

company, which he was. He could bring a dull occasion to life as soon as he entered the room. But when he was at home, he loved to be quiet and watch television, or listen to radio plays or music. He was never bored. There was always something he could find to interest him. He never tired of watching the cream of the old Hollywood movies on television, and over the years built up a great knowledge of movies and movie stars. Of all the singers in light entertainment he thought Barbra Streisand was the greatest, though she was by no means the only singer he liked listening to. Matt Monro was a friend of ours from the old days of summer seasons and Eric felt that he was one of our best singers, and rather underrated in this country. He enjoyed listening to Shirley Bassey, and Carmen McRae, who never became as popular here as in the USA, was a long-term favourite of us both. Whenever possible Eric listened to Radio 4 first thing in the morning, and he loved John Dunn's shows and Benny Green's record programme. In the car travelling to and from work he would play cassettes, among them Bing Crosby and Roger Miller.

His favourite comedian from silent films was Buster Keaton and he had great admiration for those masters of the double act, Laurel and Hardy. One of the few fan letters Eric ever wrote was to Sandy Powell of music hall fame. Another 'special' with Eric was Phil Silvers, the American comedian. He thought Phil Silvers superb, and never gave up watching repeats of his Sergeant Bilko shows. Tommy Cooper only had to look at Eric to make him laugh. I don't know how Tommy managed a serious conversation with anybody. Come to think of it, he probably didn't! His admiration for the two Ronnies had increased over the years, and Ronnie Barker and Eric stimulated each other when it came to funny lines, meeting up at various functions and dropping each other the occasional humorous letter.

Eric took enormous pleasure from classical music and composers such as Debussy and Beethoven, Ravel, Delius and Elgar. This is a side of him that few people knew. His taste in music was very varied, but he always sought quality and talent and had no interest in listening to anyone or anything he considered mediocre.

He also read a lot, and again his choice was varied. In his own special field of comedy he had a big collection of books. Many a time I remember him chuckling at a book of Billy Bennett's Monologues!

Most of us never stop learning something new all the time, and it was certainly true of Eric. Even his love of football and cricket led him to become extremely knowledgeable about the games, and his memory for names and special events was exceptional.

Although he had given up cigarettes, he carried on smoking a pipe. No picture of Eric relaxing quietly in an armchair would be complete without one of his pipes stuck between his teeth. He chewed them as much as he smoked them; it was a nervous habit, like biting your nails, and I suppose he found a pipe comforting, like a dummy. A typical Eric Morecambe pipe would not necessarily be alight but it would always be bitten at the end. He was a compulsive pipe buyer, and eventually had scores of them in the house. At times he almost couldn't go out without buying himself a new pipe. Perhaps he was slightly embarrassed by the number he got through because he used to sneak new ones in without saying anything. A few days later I would notice that he was gripping a new pipe between his teeth. If I commented on it, he would be vague and rather dismissive:

'Oh,' he'd say, 'I've had this for a while now.'

One of the little mysteries Eric left us with concerned his pipes. Just before he died he had the best of them re-stemmed, making them look as good as new. But then he decided he should give up smoking – permanently – in the hope that this would contribute to keeping him healthy. Only two days prior to his death, and just as we were going out, Eric said to our son Gary:

'You can have all my pipes, Gary, they're great now they have been re-stemmed – I'll get them for you now.' At this point he stopped in his tracks, saying: 'No, I can't give them to you now, I'll give them to you when I see you in two days' time.'

When we looked, not one single re-stemmed pipe came to light, and we haven't a clue where they could be.

Eric was never what could be termed an orderly person. He couldn't keep a diary properly, for instance; often he couldn't read his own writing, and he was forever mislaying the book! He said he was hopeless with mechanical things, and so if a fuse went he was the last person who'd be able to put it right. Once when I was away and Eric was alone in the house, the lights all went out just as it was getting dark. Eric decided that the practical thing to do was to go to bed early, which he did, then wait for daylight to come and phone for an electrician. However, he was never really quite as helpless as he made out. It was his way of getting someone else (usually me) to perform the tasks which were of no interest to him. A touch of cunning there!

Cause for celebration – Sadie and George's Golden Wedding. They held a party at a nearby hotel and invited just about everyone they had known during their married life.

He loved clothes, and the older he became the keener he was to look really smart. His main trouble with clothes was that, as he said to me, he was the only person he knew who could look wonderfully smart at ten o'clock in the morning, and a complete mess by twelve. It was true. Clothes just seemed to get crumpled faster on him than on other people.

It was the same with his wardrobe and shelves. Where other people folded their clothes and placed them in neat layers, Eric threw his into the shelves any old how, so that his sweaters and cardigans looked more like balls of wool than finished garments. Every so often he would notice this, and then he would take everything out and pile the whole lot on the bed, fold it all up and painstakingly put it back, item by item. Most people would find this a chore to do, but Eric actually enjoyed it and used to feel very proud of the end result. Three or four weeks later he would be back to square one and would go through the whole procedure again!

He used to feel a little guilty, when we were about to go on holiday, that he never helped with the packing. One year he waited until I had got everything together and then he said:

'Right. Leave the rest to me. I'll load up the car.'

He carried all the cases out of the house and put them in the car. We set off, and arrived at Heathrow Airport. We unloaded the cases and carried them inside the terminal building.

'That's funny,' I said to Eric. 'We've got one case too many.'

I looked more closely, and found that Eric had loaded an extra one that was full of jumble due to be collected the following week!

All our marriage, funny things happened to us, especially if there was a big occasion in the offing. We sometimes wondered why our life should be tinged with humour in this way, but never really hit on an answer. It wasn't as if Eric was all that accident-prone – he just needed looking after! In any case, a lot of these incidents seemed to be sprung on us by Fate, without our doing anything to make them happen.

On the day of Eric's OBE award in 1976, for instance, just when we were ready to go to Buckingham Palace, we found an injured dove in our sitting room. It must have been there since the previous morning when a window was open. Outside, the car was ready and we were all set to leave. First, however, Eric and I and Gail and Gary had to decide what to do with the dove: where should we put it so that neither cat nor dog would finish it off? Eventually we took the dove out to the stables and left it in a nice warm corner to recover. Only then were we able to set off for the Palace.

The rest of the day was memorable too. After all, it's not every day that your husband is made an Officer of the Order of the British Empire. But it's odd that our memory of the day should also feature a stranded dove!

Another time, Eric and I decided to treat ourselves to an evening out at the theatre, something we rarely did. We booked our seats and set off for the West End in Eric's Jensen. It was a dreadful evening, simply pouring with rain, so Eric dropped me off at the theatre while he went to park the car. I was almost the first person to arrive in the foyer, which rapidly filled up as the minutes ticked by. After about twenty minutes there was still no sign of Eric. I began to feel alarmed. All too soon the curtain was due to go up, and the rest of the audience vanished through the doors leading to the stalls and up the stairs to the circle, leaving me marooned in silence with the manager, who was giving me curious sidelong glances.

As I was wondering what on earth to do, a gentleman approached me saying: 'Excuse me, you are Mrs Morecambe, aren't you? I have a message from your husband.' He then explained that Eric had broken down in Leicester Square and was having to stay with the car until help arrived. With no umbrella, I set off in torrential rain to join Eric at the car. There he was, with a sorry tale to tell. It seems that when he reached Leicester Square the car suddenly stalled and stopped. Try as he might, he couldn't get the engine to restart, but fortunately – being Eric – he had broken down right outside the headquarters of the Automobile Association. Unfortunately – being Eric – the offices had closed for the night and the only person he could find in the whole building simply didn't want to know. Finally Eric persuaded this one man to phone for a breakdown vehicle to come to the rescue.

By the time the breakdown vehicle arrived, it was too late to bother about the show, in any case this bedraggled, miserable couple had lost their appetite for doing anything. We went home on the train.

Our car was taken miles away to a garage on the other side of London where it would be seen to the next day. To add insult to injury, when the next day came, a mechanic got into the car, turned on the ignition and the engine roared immediately into life! The official explanation was that the carburettor had probably flooded while Eric was trying to find a parking place. Small consolation for two frustrated theatregoers!

During the Seventies Eric and Ernie won a tremendous amount of awards, and we found ourselves regularly going to awards dinners and other functions with a show business connection. The Variety Club was always holding fund-raising lunches, dinners, and a host of other events. Eric and Ernie supported the Stars Organization for the Spastics as well, and Eric also helped the Sports Aid Foundation and the Golddiggers – he was in at their conception. After his first heart attack he began to help the British Heart Foundation, and for three years from 1977 to 1979 he was a very successful president of the Lord's Taverners, to which he gave a great deal of his time. Eric and Ernie won four awards from the Variety Club (in 1964, 1974, 1976 and 1978) and six from BAFTA (in 1964, 1969 and 1970–73); they were honoured by the Water Rats in 1970 and 1974, by the Radio Industries Organization in 1971 and 1972, and by the *Sun* newspaper in 1973 and 1974. In 1976 they received the OBE and the Freedom of the City of London, and Eric was especially proud to be awarded an honorary degree by the University of Lancaster – 'Not bad,' as he said, 'for a boy from Lancaster Road Juniors.'

The functions were not always linked to show business of course. We felt greatly honoured to be invited to dinner at the Mansion House on two occasions, and have been guests at 10 Downing Street under the occupancy of three Prime Ministers. Perhaps our greatest thrill was at being invited to a Reception at Buckingham Palace and also to one of the garden parties held annually in the grounds of the Palace. Early on in Eric and Ernie's television careers they performed for the Royal Household at Windsor Castle one Christmas and so we all enjoyed the privilege of joining in and staying to supper.

All these presentations and special occasions were marvellous, but they also meant that Eric was putting in a lot of hours at functions where he was, to all intents and purposes, working. Usually there would be a dinner, followed by speeches and perhaps a cabaret, but for Eric much of the evening was spent sitting at a table either signing autographs or talking to people who were keen to meet him. In effect, every time he went to a dinner he was making a personal appearance, and he would put one hundred per cent of himself into it. He couldn't be any different!

Many other stars would be going through a routine similar to Eric's – after all, that was how the system operated. The stars were invited because their presence at a function helped to sell lots of tickets and made the occasion a fund-raising success.

For my own part, I found that a great number of these occasions were more enjoyable in the anticipation than in the actual event. I always looked forward to going out to a big dinner or a ball. I liked to dress up for the occasion, and it was fun to meet people we didn't see very often. But often it was exhausting, and so many events seemed to crop up at a particularly busy working time.

I accepted that Eric would be largely monopolized by the other guests. We used to love dancing in our early years, but that gradually faded until finally we very rarely danced together and if we did the chances were that some other lady would come up and whisk him away. My role was to be there, but only in the background; the celebrity's wife.

Having played that role for more than twenty years, I have been surprised after Eric's death to find how much affection people have shown towards me personally. I have in no way been allowed to feel 'unwanted', and it has been a heart-warming experience. In December 1984, for instance, I was very pleased to be invited to the Children of Courage awards. This is an annual event organized by *Woman's Own* which Eric and I attended for several years and which was one of Eric's favourite events.

Each year the day began with a morning service held at Westminster Abbey, when the presentations were made to the children being honoured that day. A member of the Royal family always attended, except for one year when Mrs Thatcher did the honours. Many people contributed to giving the children a day they would always remember. After the service the usual photo session took

The Duchess of Kent sharing a joke at a Stars Organisation for Spastics Ball.

place, and the children loved having their pictures taken with the stars who were present. To round off the occasion, the children and their parents, together with a group of celebrities, had lunch at the House of Lords. Eric had a great rapport with the children, who were perfectly at home with him, and it was surprising how many little Ernie Wises he found amongst them! The final treat was the giving out of Christmas presents. I must say it seemed strange to be going to the 1984 awards without Eric, and stranger still to be asked for my autograph.

Partly, of course, it is the value of the Morecambe name which has made charities and other organizations want to keep me on as their representative. At the same time it seems that some of Eric's celebrity status has been transferred to me, which is something that I still find rather difficult to understand, however gratifying it may be. At such times I am only too glad that in my working days I had some first-hand experience of show business. Although I was only on the fringes, I too had my share of nerves and worries before a performance and this helped me enormously when it came to appreciating the pressures that a big star like Eric was subject to, and more recently to coping with public appearances now that some of Eric's limelight has fallen on me.

Back in the 'seventies one of my most important jobs was to deal with the mail and Eric's diary. He had fan mail coming in all the time, plus loads of requests from national and local organizations asking him to appear at their functions. Until you have been faced with it, you don't realize just how many clubs, societies and charities there are in Britain! It wasn't as though all the requests from, say, the British Heart Foundation, came through their central office. Organizers from the regional branches wrote in as well; so did the Rotarians and the Round Tablers, and dozens more, and it could be a big headache to decide how to reply to them. Even if Eric was willing to go to a function, we very often couldn't accept because we simply didn't know if he would be free on such and such a date. The show-business bookings obviously had to take priority, but many of these would be arranged at short notice, or else dates would be changed for reasons that were beyond our control, making it difficult to plan ahead. One of the hardest things was to explain to people who wrote to us three months in advance that we couldn't give a definite yes, even though there was nothing else in the diary for that day. People tended to think that provided they got in early enough, we would have no excuse for turning them down, whereas in effect it was often easier to accept an invitation at fairly short notice because we then knew that we were in the clear as far as television and concert dates were concerned.

Once you do commit yourself, you are carrying a big responsibility. Publicity is printed with your name on as the star guest, or letters are sent out carrying your name as the celebrity leading the appeal. If all this happens months ahead of the date, and then with a fortnight to go an attractive offer comes in for a day's work – say to film a commercial – what do you do? Well, morally you should probably stick to your original commitment, but you could also be forgiven for wishing you hadn't taken it on in the first place.

Especially around Christmas we were inundated with requests. Unfortunately, Christmas is the most stressful time of year for people in show business. Eric and Ernie always had their Christmas TV show to think of, and they also had a number of charity functions which they, along with many other performers, felt it important to support. Taken together, these dates left very little time to fit in the extra requests we received. Too many late nights, in any case, made it very difficult for Eric to be bright and sparkling, and word-perfect, if he was working the next morning.

Also at this time Eric went through a phase when he was drinking more heavily than was good for him. The trouble was, as he himself said, he was his own worst enemy. If he was at a party, he wanted to go the whole hog, and there was never any shortage of people wanting to fill up his glass.

I used to say to him: 'Put your hand over your glass next time the waiter comes round.' It never seemed to work. He was such a favourite, and gave so much of himself, that everyone wanted to look after him and top up his glass whenever it was less than about two-thirds full. The result was that in the course of a very long evening Eric would be knocking back far more than he realized.

When this phase began, I think Eric needed a little extra boost to his confidence after his heart attack and he found that an extra drink or two relaxed him. In fact, two or three Scotches would have been good for him, but once he got the taste he wanted more. He knew full well that this wasn't doing him any good, but his only remedy was to give up drinking altogether. He could always do that without difficulty, and for long periods he drank no alcohol at all, but I always thought it was a pity that he could never just cut back and get by on less. Eric, however, couldn't be a moderate.

Of all the many charity organizations which Eric supported, probably his greatest success was with the Lord's Taverners. He was the only person to serve three years as their President. Eric followed Prince Philip and Prince Charles, who each completed the usual two years in office, but they, of course, were not expected to play an active role. Eric was so outstandingly successful during his two-year term that he was asked to stay on for a third year. He enjoyed it tremendously, even though it took up a lot of his time and was often tiring. There was also a load of extra correspondence to deal with and special dates to fulfil – which also sometimes meant making speeches. Making speeches didn't come easily to Eric, though everyone assumed it did. He found them very different from his usual style of comedy, and of course nobody wanted a 'straight' speech from Eric. They looked to him for laughs and that is what he tried to give them.

In summer he had to reserve just about every Sunday for Taverners matches. Although he didn't himself play cricket, or hardly ever, he loved being at the matches as a supporter and spectator. As he wasn't contributing by playing he put in many hours in the instant-photo tent. People paid 50p a time to have a Polaroid photo taken of them with Eric. This was an ideal setting for Eric and his off-the-top humour, and he would do long spells in the tent, having a chat with every customer. Long queues used to form outside, while inside there would be lots of laughter and chuckles.

Each year the Lord's Taverners staged a ball which raised thousands of pounds for charity and was often supported by a member of the Royal Family. While he was President, Eric made a special point of making sure that his top table was filled with people who were not only friends – which also was important – but who were big attractions with the public. If you could get a good table together, so that Eric Morecambe could be seen with Ronnie Barker and Ronnie Corbett, and perhaps Elton John and Judi Dench, you could almost guarantee that the evening would get off to a good start.

One of the perks of being President of the Lord's Taverners was being invited to Lord's to watch the Test matches. Eric and I both looked forward to the luxury of seeing the game from a box, and having lunch and tea served to us.

'Of course,' Eric once said, 'you see less cricket that way.' And it

Showing all at large that they had been given the Freedom of the City of London.

was true. He would be sitting there quietly watching the match, and then someone would speak to him from behind:

'Why, Eric!'

'Oh. Hello.'

'Eric, well! Great to see you.'

'Yes, er . . .'

Huge roar from the rest of the crowd. A vital wicket has fallen – and Eric was one of the few people in the ground who missed it. Such moments strengthened his belief that the best place to watch cricket was at home on television. You can see the ball better, you get action replays if you want to look at something again, and no one distracts you while play is in progress. On the other hand, Lord's is Lord's, and neither he nor I would have wanted to exchange the experience of going there.

Memories of recent events often jostle others from long ago. On the occasion I am now thinking of, the game was not cricket, but football, which Eric used to play in all weathers for show business sides when he was doing a season. One winter, not long after we were married, we had just bought an 8-mm movie camera and Eric was due to play in a charity match. He gave me strict instructions to film as much of the action as I could.

The referee blew his whistle, and off they went, with me running up and down the touchline filming whatever I could when the players came near. I became completely absorbed in the business of capturing footballers in the viewer, and made one or two sorties out on to the pitch to get a better picture. I didn't think anyone would mind; in any case, it was meant to be a fun match for charity. However, that's not how the referee saw it. The next thing I knew, he was glaring at me and pointing somewhere into the distance. I was being ordered off!

Eric thought it was hilarious. It was no good me protesting my innocence, or saying that I had got carried away with my filming – so far as he was concerned, his wife had been sent off the field at a football match. That was the main thing, and he was absolutely delighted!

By the 'seventies, Eric was looking for more time to enjoy another favourite sport, trout fishing. Some friends of ours were also very keen on fishing and they used to go off on little trips to the country, staying in pubs or hotels and fishing the local rivers for trout and salmon.

Eric said: 'You know, I wouldn't mind having a try at that. It would make a very nice break.'

'Right,' said our friend, 'leave it to me. I'll fix up somewhere really quiet where you won't be bothered by anyone.'

This was soon after Eric had finished a television show in which Glenda Jackson had been the star guest. It was in the spring, Gail and Gary were still at school, and about to break up for Easter. Our friend booked us all into an attractive olde-worlde inn in Salisbury, and made arrangements to fish in nearby water.

We arrived in two cars and booked into the hotel, which was extremely quiet and out of the way, and later that evening down we went to dinner. We walked into the dining room – and there was Glenda Jackson along with some of the cast and film crew of *Triple Echo!* It was a most extraordinary coincidence.

It turned out that Glenda had started working on the film, which was being shot at a farmhouse near Salisbury, just after doing the Morecambe and Wise Show, and they were now almost finished. The evening in the hotel was tremendous fun, and next day, of course, instead of fishing we were down at the farmhouse watching Glenda filming. We spent the following day like that too, wandering around the farm in our wellingtons, and taking in the complexities of film making. That was the last day before the unit disbanded and went their separate ways, and Glenda gave a lovely party to which we also were invited. It was such a happy occasion and yet how ironic that, having gone all the way to the peace and quiet of Salisbury, we should end up on a film set. We all agreed that there is no getting away from show business no matter where you go!

In February 1975 Eric and I had our one and only winter holiday together. He had never been keen on going on a winter sports holiday because he felt he couldn't risk taking up skiing – something which might put him on crutches and cause a whole TV show to be cancelled.

Anyway, that year we booked ourselves ten days in Kitzbühl, though we didn't intend doing anything more physical than walking. We just wanted to enjoy a few days in the mountain air and watch others ski. The weather was magnificent, that lovely mixture of crisp deep snow and bright sunshine, and from the moment we arrived we spent as much time as we could in the open air. We took the cable car up the mountains, stayed for a while enjoying the scenery, and then came down again. Nothing strenuous, but still very invigorating.

Then we met someone called George Cochran. He was getting on a bit, but years before he had been a very successful skiing instructor. He had given up skiing and now his passion was ski-bobbing, where you ride a kind of bike mounted on skis, and small skis fit onto your boots with special pieces of metal attached for braking.

I can't quite remember how he managed to persuade us to try it, because when we got back home we were amazed that we had actually done it! All I can remember is that he had great confidence in us and made it sound so easy, so I suppose we were won over simply by that.

The first day we went up the mountain by cable-car carrying our bikes, and simply had to step out of the car through the doors. We fitted the small skis onto our boots, and turned to face the slope. George went a little way ahead, gave the signal and, taking a deep breath, we pushed off.

Earlier, he had given us brief instructions about how to manage the bobs, braking, turning, and so forth. The snag was that we had to use the same run as the skiers, and there were literally scores of them flying about the face of the mountain, which made the surface very slippery. We would have been better off in thicker snow, but it was even more dangerous to wander off on one's own, so we stayed with the pack. Although I was meant to be the athletic one, I was soon struggling. Eric, however, took to it immediately, just like a duck to water.

To my great frustration, I came off several times, mainly because I found it difficult to brake hard enough and lost control of the ski-bob. Then we hit ice. A great sheet of it, and I was in trouble. Down I went. Trying to get on again was another matter, for it was impossible to stand up and as I tried to reach for the bike it slithered out of reach. Inwardly I felt quite desperate. Then I spotted Eric who, seeing my predicament, had halted his bike, and now was very slowly trying to reach me. All the while skiers were hurtling past, narrowly missing us as I vainly tried to stay on my feet long enough for Eric to help me remount. One skier even jumped over me! Eric took it all in his stride and eventually we were on our way again. When we had finished the run and gone back to our hotel, and I had time to think about our adventure on the mountain, I remember feeling surprised that Eric had acted in the way he did. It was quite brave of him, I decided, to stop and attempt to help me in those conditions. There had been no flap, no fuss, and his ski-bob was perfectly under control as if he'd been doing it for years.

You would have thought that would be the end of our new sport, but no! George felt we were capable of bigger things – the Horn! – a much higher mountain. As George had all this confidence in us, what could we do except go? So, on the following day, with snow falling fast, the three of us set off. Eric and I hadn't realized that you don't travel up this particular mountain in a nice cosy cable car. Transport up this mountain was by chair-lift. You grab hold of a moving chair as it comes within range, hoist yourself onto it, and somehow fasten a bar across to hold you in place – while all the time you are carrying your bike! 'Impossible,' we said. 'Not at all,' said George. 'Simple!' Simple? The only thing that was simple was us for doing it!

To our astonishment we accomplished this whole tricky manœuvre without so much as a sprained wrist. But we couldn't help but notice that we were the only occupants of the chair-lift, and that there wasn't a living soul in sight on the slopes.

The snow was falling even more heavily as we prepared to launch ourselves downhill. If there was any consolation to be found it was that there would be no patches of ice to bring me down. When we were ready, George issued his final instructions. 'Whatever you do,' he said, 'stay behind me.'

Once on the move we found it far easier than on the previous day, now that we had snow beneath the ski-bobs and not ice. This is easy, I thought, as George led the way, followed by Eric with me bringing up the rear. Unfortunately, we didn't stay in that formation. With George still calling out 'Keep behind me,' I took off like a rocket at about sixty miles an hour. Past Eric and past George, who did a quick double-take when he realized that now it was me in the lead. I was absolutely petrified but knew that the most important thing was not to panic. Braking hard didn't seem to make any difference, and I was going to have to fall off sooner or later. Seeing a huge mound of snow off to my left, I altered course and drove straight into it.

Never having dived into a giant bowl of blancmange, I can't be sure it felt exactly like that, but the effect was roughly the same. When Eric and George caught up with me I was shaking off the snow. Eric should have been worried about me. But no. He was hysterical with laughter. He said it was the funniest thing he'd ever seen in his life – the sight of me clinging on like grim death and gradually fading into the distance until he could only make out my little fur hat speeding along.

Hysteria over, we all remounted and rode down to the bottom. We had never before, or since, experienced such a feeling of exhilaration and we said: 'George, it's been great. We need to have our brains examined for doing it and we shall never, ever, do it again. But thanks a million for the experience!'

10
The New Boy

Until he was eighteen, Gary was the youngest of the Morecambes. Then a small, slightly knock-kneed but very determined stranger entered our lives – Steven. Gary's new brother-to-be.

Steven came to us via our daughter Gail, who had left school and was training as a nursery nurse at a children's home in London. Now and again she used to bring children back to our house to give them a day out. They came in various shapes, sizes and colours, usually one at a time although I do remember two little black boys who were brothers and came together. It was lovely for them, and we enjoyed it too. In summer we made a point of using our swimming pool as much as we could, trying to teach them to swim.

Steven came to us more often than the others. In the beginning this was largely because he was proving quite a handful at the home and needed more care and attention than the average child in Gail's group. From the beginning he warmed to Gail and got on well with her. He had a violent temper at the age of three, when we first met him, and as we got to know him better we could see that this was really a mark of his acute frustration. As a baby he had not been loved, or played with or talked to as babies must be if they are to learn and develop. Consequently, when he was put into care Steven had almost no vocabulary beyond a small barrage of swearwords, and he was generally behind in his ability to learn and do many of the things that most other children take in their stride. At the same time he was a very alert and lively little boy, with a personality of his own, and fiercely resentful when he couldn't find words for his feelings, or his hands and fingers wouldn't do what he wanted.

One thing he did know. He liked coming to see us. He heard Gail calling her parents 'Mum' and 'Dad' and so, from the start, he did the same. When Eric and I sat together on the sofa, Steven would wriggle in between us and tuck his arms in ours, then give us all a big happy smile.

He was not only full of beans, he was full of courage too. In fact, it was probably thanks to this that he came through those bleak early years as well as he did. He had no fear of water – even before he could swim! Eric and I loved to see the children who came to our house having fun in our swimming pool, but we were always a trifle nervous that one of them would get into difficulties. Steven, especially, did little to relieve our fears. No, he would *not* wear arm bands! That was for babies. No, he would *not* wear a ring round his middle!

He ended up teaching himself to swim in a way that was completely his own. He watched the older boys – Gary and his friends – to see what they did, and copied them. To begin with, he could only keep himself above the surface for a couple of strokes before he started to sink. That didn't worry him in the slightest. To our horror, his method was to jump into the deep end, push himself off the bottom and, when he broke the surface, take a big breath and swim for all he was worth, imitating the strokes of the bigger boys. When he felt himself sinking, he simply let himself go down, bounced off the bottom, broke surface again – another deep breath, swim like mad, sink, bounce, up again ... and so on until he gradually got the hang of staying on the surface.

We took him to Portugal with us when he was still very young. One day on the beach we looked round for him, and suddenly he wasn't there. We thought he couldn't be very far away, but there was no sign of him. Just along the beach from us was a tent. We went along and looked inside. A Portuguese family, mother, father and several little children, were sitting in a circle round a camp stove cooking sardines. One little boy was paler than the others – and guess who that was. Independent as ever, Steven had made friends with the other children and tagged along when they went off to lunch. They couldn't understand a word he said, and vice versa, but they all got on like a house on fire – and he thoroughly enjoyed tucking into their sardines!

The head of the table for Steven on his sixth birthday. I was impressed at not one glass of lemonade being split.

His bad language surfaced on many occasions before he learned to control it, but in the beginning swearwords were a normal part of his vocabulary as well as something to be used when he was angry. One day in Portugal, we were joined at our villa by Dickie Davies and his family. They were over by the pool together and Dickie was helping to teach Steven to swim. As usual, Steven jumped into the deep end, then thrashed his way to the side. He gripped the edge of the pool, then shook himself and looked up at Dickie.

'F——— cold in here, isn't it, Dickie,' he said in a cheerful voice. Dickie was flabbergasted at this tiny mite coming out with such a word.

Even though Steven had been coming to us for some while, and we were all very fond of him, it came as a great surprise when the authorities asked us if we would foster him on a permanent basis. We considered this carefully, but decided we couldn't possibly go ahead. We knew almost no details of Steven's original home background, except that he hadn't been cared for, and fostering could have laid us open to all kinds of problems, especially with Eric being such a well-known personality. Parents had the right to turn up at the house, or, much worse, suddenly decide they'd like Steven back after all and take him off to resume the life he had got away from.

We thought it would be most unfair to Steven, especially after he had been exposed to our way of life, which is comfortable and, some might say, luxurious. Suddenly to pull a child away from that environment and thrust him into another, very different one might do irreparable harm. Fostering was not a sensible thing to do in our case, and so we turned down the request.

The authorities digested this for a while, and then came back with another suggestion. This time they asked us to consider adopting Steven as our own son. They pointed out that Steven identified himself with our family and if we said no there was little hope for him; he would spend the rest of his childhood and youth living in homes.

Making up our minds about Steven was one of the biggest decisions Eric and I ever took. There was no question of lack of affection. We both loved him, and so did Gary and Gail. But was it not too late? There was such a gap in age between our grown-up children and this little boy. Also, we lived such a hectic life because of Eric's work, could we really give Steven the attention and stability that he obviously needed? Even if we thought we could, did we really want to? At this stage, after twenty years of married life, Eric and I were looking forward to less, not more, responsibility in regard to our children. In a way we felt we had served our time worrying about our children and their education and being tied by school schedules. Like most parents, our own desires had come last for a long time and we quite looked forward to having more freedom for ourselves.

Then we looked at Steven. We thought, how can we shut the door in his face? What possible chance had he got without us? We looked at each other. Eric said:

'Hell's bells. We've got so much, we've been so fortunate. Let's have him.'

Gail and Gary also wanted Steven. They both loved him, and Gary was already like a second or younger father to him, deputizing for Eric in the roughhouses and being on permanent call for games of football in the garden. Eric was nevertheless careful to point out that if Steven joined the family he would be a full member, and that meant a three-way share-out among the children. Gail and Gary were not deterred. So the three of them all voted in favour, then they said to me:

'We're for having Steven, but the final decision has got to be yours because in the end it is you who will have to do all the work.'

What was I to say, except yes. I felt under no particular pressure from the others, who were simply stating their feelings and also admitting quite honestly that they didn't occupy the key position that I did. On the other hand, I know that if I had said no, and shut the door on him, it would have haunted me all my life. In any case, from his first day with us, Steven had looked around, weighed us all up – and adopted us. We had better do the same for him!

So it was decided, and Steven became a member of the family. It did mean sacrifices, and difficulties, but we would have been kidding ourselves if we hadn't expected them. Any child from such a background is by normal standards disturbed, and needs a lot of love and attention. At the age of four and five, Steven could not do things that most other children could. Although he was very outgoing and gregarious, he had a lot of problems with reading, which would hold him back in various school subjects.

We thought at first he was dyslexic, but he wasn't. What he had was a form of word-blindness and we arranged for him to have special remedial lessons at the house – which he resisted. However, when he went to Beechwood, the local prep school, he was very happy. He settled in quickly, but still needed special remedial teaching. Gradually over the years he calmed down and his old fears left him.

For a long time he was uneasy at night, and didn't want to be left on his own. Steven wanted more than anything to come into bed with me and Eric and spend the whole night with us. Eric was equally determined that he should not.

'It's the one thing I'm going to be firm about,' he said. 'If he once gets into bed with us it'll be every night. We'll never be able to keep him out.'

Steven slept at one end of a long passage, and our bedroom was at the other end. He had a night light in his room, and we also kept a

My favourite Christmas photograph – Steven was by this time fully adopted and Gail and Paul home safe and sound from their African Safari.

landing light burning for him. When he was a very little boy, he would come down the passage, stand for a while in the open doorway, then try to sneak into bed with us. Night after night we said no, he could get into our bed in the morning and have a little cuddle, but he had to go to sleep first in his own bed.

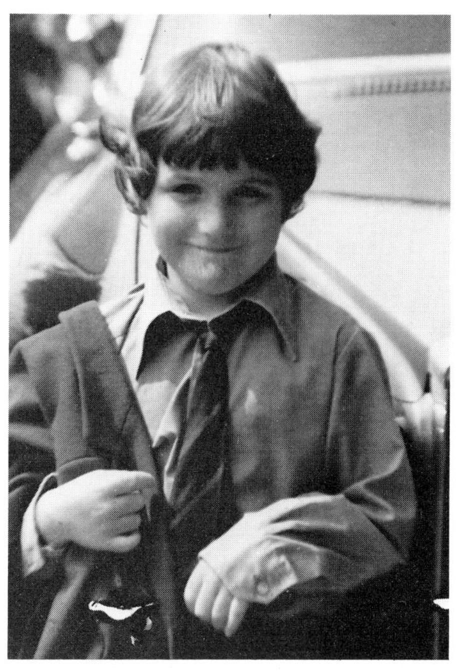

RIGHT Just William? No, just Steven. A typical schoolboy arriving home from school at the end of a hard day's play!

As a kind of compromise, whenever he came into us, I would go back with him to his room, and sit reading him stories until he went to sleep. Like most children of that age he loved being read to, and it was a nightly ritual at bedtime. In his case it was especially important and not something to be rushed and got over with as quickly as possible. Many a time I've been the one to drop off to sleep half-way through a sentence, and had to be woken up by a very wide-awake Steven prompting me!

At times I felt as if I was a female buffer keeping two inflexible males apart. Some nights I would hear a noise in the passage, and go out and find Steven sitting on the carpet halfway between his room and ours. He knew that we wouldn't let him stay in our room, but he was determined not to give in, and ended up stubbornly sitting on the floor outside until I rescued him. Even when he was four years old, Steven showed that he was a great survivor. He didn't actually win the battle of the beds – in fact I think he just grew out of his fear of being alone at night – but my goodness he showed what a fighter he could be.

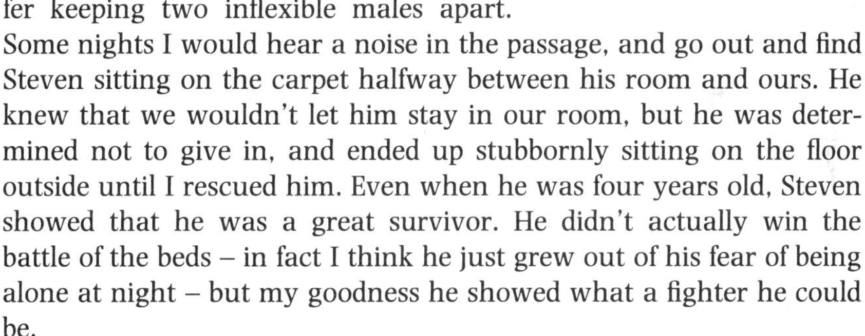

Today, Steven has filled out remarkably, and is almost unrecognizable as an older version of the knock-kneed little lad who first came to see us on a day out from the children's home. Eric used to say he was built like a brick chicken house! He is now as tall as me – and I am taller than most! – and very happy at his Quaker boarding school. He is extremely interested in country sports such as shooting and fishing, and thinks he might like to take up forestry for a living, or become a gamekeeper or go into farming.

Quite where all this enthusiasm for the great outdoors came from I have never been sure, but Steven has always been a great one for going off on long walks, and for climbing and generally making his own way from one place to the next. One springtime we were in Portugal when Steven must have been about twelve. He went off on a walk early in the morning, and by lunchtime he hadn't returned. The afternoon went by and still he hadn't come back. I was getting really worried, and my mother, who was also with us at the villa, was in a cold sweat. I tried to reassure her.

'Don't worry,' I told her. 'I'm sure he's all right. You know what Steven's like. I expect he's walked such a long way, he's probably stopped on the way back for a Coke, or he's met someone on the beach and is talking to them.'

I wished I felt as confident as I tried to sound. But where on earth had he got to?

About five o'clock, we saw this utterly weary figure dragging itself up the garden towards us. He was absolutely filthy, his clothes were caked in goodness knows what, and he certainly didn't smell like the nice fresh Steven we had said goodbye to that morning.

'What have you been doing? Where have you been?'

'Oh,' he said. 'I followed that dried-up river bed for a few miles until I came to a farm. The farmer there was having terrible trouble because all his ewes had started giving birth and there was only him and his wife to do the work. So I stopped and gave him a hand. And that's what I've been doing – lambing.'

'You mean you've been there all day, on this farm?'

'Yes,' said Steven, 'and it was really hard work. I was tired out long before we finished. But the farmer was so pleased with me, he took me back to his house and gave me a glass of wine.'

'You mean you've been drinking wine? On an empty stomach?'

'Oh,' he said, 'I did have this lump of bread as well as the wine. I drank about half a bottle.' He gave us a little grin.

I said: 'Do you realize how dangerous that was? You've had all that wine, and then you've walked back along the clifftop. You could have gone over the edge!'

'Well,' he said, 'to tell you the truth, I really felt drunk coming home. Then I was sick as anything, and after that I felt all right.'

No wonder he was in the state he was. Although he was just about exhausted, I made him take off all his filthy clothes and give himself a good bath and clean-up. I have since wondered if that day out in Portugal was an early sign that he wanted to be a farmer!

We formally adopted Steven in 1974. The next three years were to be a time of many changes in our family – changes that were only to be expected, I suppose, given the ages of those involved, but changes that brought us a sharp mixture of joy and sadness.

Gail was already engaged to be married when she began bringing Steven home. Soon she and her fiancé, Paul, were to go off on an expedition to Africa. It had been carefully planned and saved up for over a period of two years by Paul and a group of friends at university. They wanted to take three Land Rovers across to Morocco and go on a safari south through the Sahara and across the centre of Africa, ending up in Kenya where the parents of one of the other young men lived.

The prospect initially caused Eric and me many misgivings, because Gail up to then had led a rather sheltered life and, however carefully planned the journey was, there would still be an element of danger. At the same time, she was coming up to twenty-one and was quite capable of taking important decisions for herself. She was reaching the end of her training period as a nursery nurse, and Paul was on the point of finishing at university, so it was an ideal time for them to go off on a big adventure together, something they would remember for the rest of their lives.

The expedition was scheduled to set off in August, and as the time grew near for final preparations it was decided (by them!) that our paddock would be an ideal place to assemble, do the final work on the vehicles and finally pack up and leave. So that is what they did. We were taken over! The place filled up with the Land Rovers and all their bits and pieces and spare parts, and the paddock suddenly became a hive of industry with the youngsters working up to the last minute.

Suddenly they were ready. Eric and I stood outside our front gates, together with friends and relatives of the others in the group, and watched in a kind of fascinated amazement as the three Land Rovers drove out of the paddock and set off in the general direction of Africa.

Outwardly, all we could do was put on bright smiles and wave madly until they were out of sight, while in our hearts we wondered why on earth we had allowed it to happen.

Quite apart from the prospects of physical danger and the likelihood of health problems along the way, I was also sorry that Gail would not be at home for her twenty-first birthday. As it happened, she and the others were lost in the desert on that great day, and Gail was also stricken with dysentery which affected them all in the course of the journey. She will never forget her twenty-first, but

They look as if they mean business! No turning back now. Gail, Paul and Co. all set to motor to Africa.

not in the way we had always expected! Anyway I am glad to be able to say that they all survived these and other tribulations, such as having to prevent various border guards from relieving them of their cash and belongings, and they eventually reached their destination. After a few days' rest they all flew home in December. Seeing them safe and sound was the best Christmas present we could have had.

On 6 September 1975 Gail and Paul were married. The day before the wedding, we suffered the anxiety of Eric waking up partially

Eric escorting Gail to the church on her wedding day. She was quite overcome for the moment seeing all the people who had come to wish her well.

paralyzed – the effects of which I explain in more detail in the next chapter. The wedding itself, and the reception at a hotel in St Albans, went off beautifully with the sun shining brightly from early morning until evening. All of Harpenden seemed to turn out to see us arriving at the church and a wonderful joyous atmosphere prevailed the whole day. Our only sadness at the time was that George, Eric's father, was ill in Morecambe and he and Sadie were unable to come to their only granddaughter's wedding, which I know they had desperately wanted to do.

Around that time we had become friendly with Graham Hill, the racing driver, and his family, who had a magnificent home only about twenty minutes' drive from us. Graham had started to give large parties which were always lovely events with lots of interesting guests. On 24 November a dinner party in honour of Graham was held at the Cafe Royal in London and Eric was asked to make one of the speeches. His speech was both relaxed and funny – and went down extremely well with Graham and the other guests. This was just as well because Graham himself had a reputation as a very gifted speaker, a natural who could be fluent and entertaining with not a note in sight.

Only days later, Eric and I were sitting at home watching the late news on television. There was an item about an aircraft that had crashed on landing at Elstree. Our thoughts flew to Graham because we knew he had been away with his racing team, and only too soon it was confirmed that it was his plane, and he and his companions were all lost in the disaster – a terrible shock for us who knew him, and his family, as friends.

No sooner had we got over that blow when, on 2 January, the phone rang. It was Sadie, sounding utterly bewildered. She told us that George was dead.

It had been quite sudden. He had got up from his armchair, and said: 'Come on, Sadie. We're off to bed,' and collapsed and died instantly.

The effect on Sadie was profound, and from that day she lost much of her old drive. It was as though she saw that her life was now virtually at an end and all she really looked forward to was being reunited with George. For a while she came to stay with us, but then she went back to Morecambe and moved to a small bungalow.

Eric's fiftieth birthday on 14 May 1976 was a most memorable day. We had planned to celebrate by going to see Roy Castle in a show and then having a meal together afterwards, so we were quite unprepared for all the extra attention we received during the day. At the theatre Roy and everyone in the show were tremendous to Eric. They filled a tray with presents for him and made a great fuss of us, which we both loved.

However, the biggest surprise happened earlier, during the afternoon. Eric and I were sitting at home when there was a knock at the door. We could hear the hubbub of voices, and when we went to see who it was – there, to our complete amazement, stood all our neighbours holding a birthday cake for Eric. Without a word to me or anyone in our family, they had found out it was Eric's fiftieth birthday and then banded together to produce this wonderful cake with candles, plus some bottles of champagne.

It was a good job we were at home and able to invite them inside! I remember we said to them: 'This is fantastic. We never dreamed we were going to have a champagne party at teatime and it's absolutely great. Unfortunately, we're going to have to throw you out in about an hour because we've got to go to London.'

So that's what we did. We had a short but very jolly party, cut the cake and drank champagne. The weather was fine and we were able to go out in the garden, as well as show our neighbours all the loads of cards and telegrams that had been arriving for Eric since morning. The funny thing was that although we hadn't planned to do all that much about his fiftieth birthday, the rest of the world had taken a completely different view – and given us a day that will always linger in my memory.

Another birthday which has stayed in my mind – though for rather different reasons – was Gary's twenty-first the following year. Gary had asked us if he could depart from the pattern of the big family get-together and have something smaller and informal. He fancied inviting just a few friends from the Further Education College in St Albans where he had been doing a course in business studies. In the end, at the very last minute, we fell between all the stools and had half the family plus loads of friends, and wished that we'd hired the rugby club or somewhere more suitable for all the young people to let off steam, which was what I'd wanted to do in the first place!

The day also had its sad side. Not long before, Sadie had been very ill in hospital in Lancaster and we had brought her down to Harpenden to recuperate. While she was with us, she was again taken ill and had to go into hospital in Harpenden, where she stayed for several days. In the ambulance coming back to us she had a stroke, which at first we weren't aware of, and subsequently she suffered a second stroke.

The day of Gary's party came, and although with Sadie upstairs we felt we should be going around on tiptoe and not having any celebrations, we went ahead and everyone duly came and enjoyed themselves.

For many days Sadie fought to keep going. Despite her sadness over the loss of George, while with us she gave no sign that she wanted anything more than to be with her only son and his family.

She battled to the end and talked and talked, mainly about the old days, going on right through the night and dozing off only occasionally; getting events confused but still struggling to express herself. During the days when she was confined to bed, I used to kiss her goodnight every night. On one occasion, when it seemed she was past knowing, I started to tiptoe out of the room without doing so.

'Joan,' said a quiet voice, 'will you kiss me goodnight?'

It moved me deeply and made me aware of how elderly people crave a demonstration of affection.

This was during a period when Eric was away from home quite frequently doing concerts, and it fell to me to nurse Sadie during her illness. Eventually, after many nights with hardly any sleep, I enlisted the help of a nurse living locally and she came in and shared the duties with me. Soon after Gary's party Eric was away for three days and Sadie, we knew, was nearing the end. She wouldn't give in, though, and we began to sense that she was waiting for Eric.

He arrived back on the Sunday after a concert in Manchester. He went up to see Sadie, and as he went through the door she turned to look at him, and breathed her last. It was as though, in that last spell of her illness, she had been hanging on just for Eric, to see him one final time.

11
'What Are You Doing This Afternoon?'

If I could erase a year from our lives, that year would be 1979. Not only was it the most critical time for Eric, culminating in his triple-bypass operation at Harefield Hospital, almost everything we tried to do went wrong.

January began pleasantly enough. On 7 January Amelia, our first grandchild, was christened and we had a big family party at the house. The christening was held at the church where Gail and Paul were married, and afterwards we came back and celebrated. Everyone seemed full of optimism and it was a joyous start to the New Year.

Less than two weeks later, Eric was taken ill and had to go into the Coronary Care Unit at St Albans Hospital. He came home after four days, on the twenty-third, with instructions to take things very quietly and spend several days in bed. On his first evening back, he was settled in bed upstairs and I was just going out of the room when he told me I looked worn out. I said I'd be all right, I'd sit around for a bit downstairs and then take Barney, our golden retriever, for his late-night walk.

'Why don't you take Barney now,' said Eric. 'Take him now and then you can have an early night. You'll feel better for it in the morning.'

It was true that I did feel exhausted after everything that had happened. Gary was living with us at the time, but he was out having dinner with friends and planned to stay the night in case he wanted more than a glass or two of wine, so there was no reason why I shouldn't take Eric's advice and go to bed early. It was barely half-past nine when I put Barney on the lead and out we went.

Heavy snow had fallen for days and lay thick on the ground. It

One of many happy photos taken at Amelia's christening.

was a beautiful night with not a breath of wind and that strange unnatural hush which accompanies snowy weather. There seemed not a sign of life apart from Barney and me, and the only disturbance in the snow was from our footprints. Having left the house behind us we turned the corner and proceeded on one of our familiar routes – up the Avenue, circle round the spinney, and then return home. Slowly we picked our way through the deep snow.

Ahead of us, as we neared the top of the road, I could see a couple out walking their dog. They had let it off the lead and this worried me a little because I was already having to restrain Barney, who is no lightweight and was pulling towards the other dog. Not knowing if it was friendly, I decided to quicken my stride and try to avoid meeting up with it.

I came to a house where the owners had cleared the snow from their drive right up to the kerbside. Unfortunately, they hadn't salted or sanded the surface and, unbeknown to me, it was lethal – a solid sheet of ice. I stepped onto it; up went my feet and down went I with an awful thud! As I lay there I found that suddenly my left ankle filled my wide, loose-fitting boot ... and that couldn't be right! The couple with the dog came over and offered to help. We first tried knocking on the door of the house. No reply. Either they were out or they didn't hear. So then the couple rushed off to their own house to fetch their car.

They were back quickly and took Barney and me home. It turned out that the wife was a trained nurse and she kindly offered to help, either by dressing the ankle or driving me to St Albans Hospital. There was an ambulance strike on at the time so, what with that and the weather conditions, to be driven in privately would be a great help. It was really very kind of them. But I felt choked with anxiety over how Eric was going to take all this; besides, he couldn't be left in the house all by himself.

There are times when one makes all the wrong decisions, and this was one of them. I let the couple go. I crawled up the stairs and, as quietly as possible, hopped along the passage leading to our bedroom. As I reached the half-closed door a voice said:

'Well, what have you done then?'

That man – how did he always know when something was wrong?

'It's all right,' I squeaked back, 'I've just hurt my ankle a bit.'

Eric was sitting up in bed, as calm as you like, with no sign of getting agitated, thank goodness.

'You've really done yourself an injury, haven't you?' he said. 'Right. No arguing. Ring for the doctor.'

Feeling terrible at having to drag the doctor out in such weather, I phoned. I needn't have worried, the doctor was also unwell and didn't feel up to coming out. He promised to come first thing in the morning and in the meantime I phoned my next-door neighbour who, like my rescuer, was a trained nurse. Robin, who was both friend and neighbour, soon let herself into the house and made her way to the bedroom. At this point I realized that we had all the ingredients for an M & W sketch, for Robin had also fallen and sprained her ankle. She had already bandaged herself, and now set about fixing me up for the night.

Next morning the doctor came and, finding that I had a fracture, phoned for an ambulance. In spite of the strike, one shortly arrived and up trouped the ambulance men with a stretcher. They eyed first Eric, then me, and were assured that yes, it was me this time.

St Albans Hospital was one mass of people with sprained and broken legs, arms, ankles, wrists and elbows. 'What a naughty girl you are, not sending for the ambulance last night,' scolded the nursing sister. 'We could have seen to you right away then. Now we are so busy.'

There was no answer to that! It was four o'clock in the afternoon before the ankle was X-rayed, found to be fractured in three places, and set, and the only available space for doing the setting was the operating theatre. While I was waiting and worrying about how Eric and I were going to get through the next few weeks, I couldn't help thinking: 'My God, life can be cruel.' What's more, as Eric often said, it *is* all based on timing!

For reasons unknown, this was also the time we had picked to have our kitchen gutted and completely refitted. It had taken us twelve years to face up to the thought of all that upheaval, but now the decision had been made.

One end of the kitchen had a low ceiling with concealed lighting set in it to shine down on the breakfast table. We had always thought it was a simple decorative ceiling, with no hidden secrets. Wrong! As soon as the builders started to pull it down, there were ominous sounds of 'What have we here then?'

What in fact we had there, concealed behind the ceiling, were the supporting beams that held up a large part of the house. If they were taken out, new beams would be needed. No problem at all, madam. No, not if you don't mind the builders now moving in on the bedroom above and taking up carpets and floor boards in order to lay the new beams.

We could have, should have, cancelled the whole thing before they even began, but we didn't. Our lovely dining room started to look like a battlefield, with all the goods from the kitchen moved in there. I also wonder if I qualify for the *Guinness Book of Records* as the only woman to cook meals on a calor gas camping stove in the middle of a traditionally furnished dining room while standing on one leg! We came through it with only one further disaster. Having painstakingly cooked a Boeuf Bourguignon in a Pyrosil dish, I dropped it en route to the living room – which was where we ate – and it smashed to pieces. No dish, no dinner! A few tears flowed at this stage. My Long John Silver walk was no help at all when it came to carrying hot dishes of food. Eric said I only needed a parrot on my shoulder!

At last it was done, the builders left and the rest of February passed fairly quietly, then in March I had a very unpleasant attack of gastro-enteritis. I was violently sick too many times to count, and spent the day lying in bed just praying that I had brought up my last and would soon begin to recover. At about ten in the evening I still felt extremely ill and reluctantly we phoned for the doctor. He was quite horrified when he saw me and told us off for being so slow to send for him. He gave me an injection and did what he could to make me more comfortable.

'Look,' he said, 'if you get any worse, make sure you give me a ring. Don't worry about calling me out in the night, you just give me a ring.'

'Yes,' I whispered, 'thank you.' Already I was feeling a lot better.

The doctor went downstairs. Eric offered him a Scotch and they sat around talking for a while. Eventually Eric came up to bed, and we settled down to a reasonably comfortable night.

There was no way that I could rise and shine the next morning, but Gary had already arranged with me that he would call Steven on time, give him his breakfast, and take him to catch his school bus. Nobody thought to involve Eric in this and so it came as a surprise to the two lads when they suddenly found themselves joined by Dad, who felt he should be lending a hand.

Gary and Steven were in the next room eating their toast when Eric went to the fridge and opened the door. There was a crash and Gary rushed in to find Eric lying on the floor clutching the remains of a roast chicken in his hands. For a moment he thought Eric was joking, but then he saw the chalk-white face and beads of sweat, and knew this was no joke.

'What happened?' Eric stammered as he was helped to his feet.

'You fainted,' Gary answered, and noticed that Eric's heart was pounding wildly. He quickly phoned for the doctor and then with great difficulty assisted Eric up the stairs where he collapsed on the bed next to me. Now there were two of us lying there with faces whiter than the sheets. Comedy is very close to tragedy at times.

The doctor soon arrived but it was a few seconds before he realized that I wasn't the patient. This time it was Eric, with whom he had been chatting and laughing only a few hours previously.

One quick examination was all that was needed. An ambulance was sent for and arrived in record time. The ambulancemen were becoming used to seeing both Eric and me in bed, looking ghastly. Then Eric was driven off at breakneck speed with a very worried doctor aboard. He asked Gary to follow behind in his car.

The house was now deathly quiet, and I lay there waiting with a feeling of complete helplessness and frustration. Surely these things only happened in books, not in real life.

Eric weathered this heart attack, but the doctors were concerned about him and needed to find out what was causing him such problems. They obviously had a pretty good idea, but Eric first had to get his strength back and then undergo more examinations and tests than he had ever had before. It was now eleven years since his first major attack, and, as we began to realize, damage done to the heart is irreversible.

After tests at both Harefield Hospital and in London, including an angiogram and scan, the moment of decision came. On 29 May Eric and I were sitting in a little room at Harefield Hospital with Dr Towers and Magdi Yacoub, the famous heart surgeon.

Mr Yacoub said: 'Eric, we've looked at all the evidence and seen the results of the tests, and our recommendation is that you should have a bypass operation.'

I sat there feeling stunned, and then blurted out: 'Do you think we should get a second opinion?'

Eric laughed so much over that remark, and never let me forget it.

'Second opinion,' he said. 'You've just been talking to the top heart surgeon in the country, probably the world! Who else is there?'

After hearing the advice, Eric asked what would happen if he didn't have the operation.

'We wouldn't expect you to live more than a few months,' was the reply.

'What are you doing this afternoon?' asked Eric.

The die was cast. Eric was very calm about it, as he always was when faced with a real crisis. I must confess that I was shocked by the news, and to begin with found it hard to accept. Ever since the first heart attack in 1968 we had been sensible about Eric's condition. We did not question that he had to stop smoking and might have to take pills for the rest of his life. Eric adapted very well to these new disciplines, and although at the back of his mind, and mine, there was a constant fear – which in effect was an extra stress – that he might have another heart attack if he went on working, as the years went by it seemed as though he had made a complete recovery. Perhaps we were naïve to assume this.

At his various checkups this attitude was always encouraged, and it is true that a long time had passed by before he began to experience further problems. Even then, it did not occur to us that because he was getting older his heart must be deteriorating.

Before the attacks of 1979 there had been warning signs. On the day before Gail's wedding, in September 1975, Eric had felt unwell and, amid all the preparations for the wedding of our only daughter, with floods of people expected at the house, he knew something was definitely wrong and we had to leave everything and go to the doctor. He had woken up feeling numb down his left side and couldn't control his arm or leg properly. It felt like a kind of paralysis and he wondered if he had had a stroke. The doctor told him that he had had a spasm of a blood vessel, and that he should cancel all immediate work. Eric, who was so keen for the wedding to be a wonderful day, decided to use a walking-stick to help him keep his balance. In answer to questions from the press, who were there in large numbers, he explained the stick away by saying that he had had a fall. Although he did drop the stick and it fell with a clatter as he stood at the altar with Gail, he picked it up again and got through the day without any further problems. When we returned home after the reception, along with many friends and family, Eric and Billy Marsh had a quiet but serious talk about the immediate show dates which were fixed. Already they had cancelled a Sunday concert scheduled for the next day.

To return to 1979, Eric went down to Hampshire to stay with Dickie and Liz Davies for a few days before he went to Harefield, and do some fishing. Each night he and Dickie sat up talking until the early hours. One night they carried on until three o'clock in the morning – nothing very deep but Eric was obviously apprehensive about the operation and needed company. The talking had to stop, however, because by then it was Saturday morning and if Dickie hadn't got some sleep he would have been in no condition to drive to London and present *World of Sport* in a few hours' time.

In discussions with me, Eric was very clear about his attitude to the future. 'I'm not afraid to die', he said. 'If I go, then I shan't know anything about it. I'll have the injection and the happy pills, and that will be that. It's you and the family who will suffer, because you will have to carry on without me. I know you will grieve for me, and I want to be missed and remembered, but I don't want there to be any long faces. If I don't get through this operation, I don't want you to spoil your life because of me.'

We had immense support from the public. Thousands of letters arrived to wish Eric well, and it was a great comfort to both of us to sit together and read them. I think it is true to say that only a few entertainers in every generation catch the public sympathy in such a big way. Out of all the mail we received, only one letter was upsetting. It arrived while Eric was in hospital waiting to have his operation the next day, and said: 'I hope you die'. We shrugged it off saying that, with so many letters, you had to allow for one crank or nutter to write in.

The operation was a complete success, although it left Eric in considerable pain for some while and physically weakened for much longer. By now, of course, he possessed by far the most famous heart in Britain, and its progress was monitored in great detail by the press and on radio and television. It never ceased to puzzle us that the state of his health should be followed with concern by virtually the whole nation. Eric reacted to this in typical fashion, asking if he could borrow a plastic heart from the hospital so he could pull some dreadful stunt on the day he left. I seem to recall he was dissuaded from carrying that idea through, and the public at large were also denied a view of his new scars – though for a 'privileged' few he would show them off, crying: 'The mark of Zorro is upon me!'

When he came out of Harefield, the press and television cameras were all there, and Eric gave one of those sparkling interviews which tended to leave people amazed that anyone could be so funny and apparently so casual about his own well-being, even after a life-saving operation. Yet somehow Eric always managed to conceal his deeper emotions and on the spur of the moment would find something witty and original to say to the waiting journalists. They could never have known just how much he would have loved to slip quietly away without any fuss. I think many people recognized that he was

'Harefield Healthy Heart Run' has become an annual event. It makes a lot of money for the fund and at the same time everyone thoroughly enjoys themselves. Even Magdi Yacoub makes time to join in.

actually making an extraordinary effort, and were moved at the same time as they laughed at his jokes. It was one of the many sides of Eric that made him special.

When he came home he was looking forward to carrying on with a book he had been writing. While he had been living quietly before the operation he had written several chapters of his first novel, *Mr Lonely*, and in Harefield he told one of the doctors about it and how much he was looking forward to taking it up again. He was surprised when the doctor said:

'Eric, you may not be able to, at least not for a while. You'll find that you have no concentration.'

The doctor was right, and Eric was rather frustrated by this, but the operation has such a profound effect on the mind as well as the body that the patient has no reserve of energy to spare for other activities, so it was a few weeks before he could hold his concentration long enough to carry on with the novel.

On 14 August our local doctor came to give Eric a check-up. He had just entered the house when the phone rang. It was a friendly journalist ringing to say he thought Eric and I should know that my brother Alan was reported lost at sea in the Fastnet Race. This was the year of the freak storms when huge seas played havoc with the race and seven people lost their lives.

We spent the rest of that day in a state of dreadful suspense, not able to think about anything else; every minute seemed like an hour. After the doctor left, having examined Eric and said he was getting on fine, we sat around the house with nothing to do but wait for further news. On this occasion – and there have been others! – the press were very good and considerate towards us. They knew full well that the emergency numbers would be engaged the whole day, so they kept us in touch with any developments as soon as they heard about them. At long last they rang to say that Alan had been found and airlifted to safety after spending the night in the sea. What a relief – but sadly two of the crew drowned.

After Eric and I had heard the news about Alan, we shook our heads and wondered where disaster would strike next. It seemed as though 1979 would never end.

12
Winding Down

After Eric's operation at Harefield Hospital, he had a period of rest and recuperation and then was back working hard again. In February 1980 he and Ernie began rehearsals for a new TV series and I went to most recordings of the programmes. Although the shows were now spaced out more than they had been, each one was extremely hard work. Once Eric began a series he never really got it out of his mind until all the shows were finished. This was even more true now, because it was a constant struggle to come up with new material. Not only Eric and Ernie, but Eddie Braben too was finding it that much harder to produce lines that would make people laugh.

This is in no way a criticism of any of them. Eddie, for instance, had been marvellous for Morecambe and Wise for more than ten years, but as the years go by it does become harder to maintain a high standard. All their lives Eric and Ernie had enjoyed their careers, and it was only in the last few years, with the anxiety about Eric's health plus the difficulty of finding new material, that a lot of the pleasure went out of working – for Eric anyway. Not only was it becoming more of an effort, it took more out of him.

In the meantime, Eric kept up his work for the Lord's Taverners and went to several cricket matches where he'd sign autographs in aid of the charity, or do spells in the Polaroid tent. The fixture at Blenheim Palace was always a favourite with its magnificent setting – and a few sideshows for Steven, who most years won a goldfish to add to his growing fleet. 'They'll never live,' we used to tell him, but they always did, and now reside indoors in their own aerated tank. The Blenheim match was held on Whit Sunday, and somehow it worked out that Eric was usually free on that day. Ironically, in 1984, we hadn't noted it in our diary, and when Stan Stennett asked if Eric would appear in his show at Tewkesbury, we said yes, never giving a thought to Blenheim.

In July 1980 we both went to Guernsey for the Taverners. Everyone on the trip stayed with a Taverner and his family. The weather was outstandingly dreadful and on the morning of the match we watched with gloom as the rain came bucketing down, filling up our host's terrace and then seeping into the house. 'There is no way they'll ever play today,' we said, prepared to bet all our worldly goods on a wash-out. And yet they did. An hour before the match was due to start, the rain miraculously stopped and then the teams and the organisers literally worked like navvies to sweep and drain the pitch so they could play on it. A wonderful effort by all – but then, as I well know, you should never underestimate a cricket nutter once he has set his mind on playing!

Also during the year we fitted in a number of work-cum-social dates. For several years running we went to Sir Billy Butlin's charity weekend in Jersey. Each year he would arrange for a member of the Royal Family to attend, and on this occasion the royal guests were the Duke and Duchess of Kent and with them Lord and Lady Romsey. Two years previously we were honoured to have Lord Mountbatten, a charming man who made a marvellous witty speech. Various celebrities would be asked to give their services for a concert, which was the high spot of the weekend. Marvellous shows they were too. There would be a golf tournament, and luncheon and dinner parties. They were the most superbly organized occasions and a real pleasure to go to because they treated us so well.

As usual between May and September, Eric went trout fishing on the Test whenever he could get away. Usually he would drive himself there and back in a day, which made it a rather strenuous outing but he preferred it that way to staying overnight. He played his tapes in the car and always took it easy on the road, then when he got there he didn't have to worry about someone else having to hang about all day while he went off to fish. Unless he was with a friend, he didn't want anyone else tagging along while he walked the bank in search of trout.

1974. The British Heart Foundation took this picture on a visit to our home. Our 'almost new' son, Steven, had a T shirt given to him.

Another very pleasant date for us was the Metropolitan Police Horse Show. We had become friendly with David McNee, who was Commissioner of Police at the time, and he and his wife Isabel invited us to several functions. We were late for lunch, I remember, completely stuck in the traffic and unable to move for half an hour or more. '*Us*,' we shouted to each other, as we fumed away in the car.

'We who are late for nothing!' When we got there at last, we entered the marquee to find all the other guests sitting down to lunch.

'It's all the police's fault, you know,' said Eric with a grin at Commissioner McNee. 'Where were they when the traffic needed sorting out?'

There was no answer to that!

Once a month, regular as clockwork, the filming of another Morecambe and Wise Show was completed and stored, ready for transmission. Eric also made appearances in a couple of short films, based on John Betjeman's works. The producer, Charles Wallis, had invited Eric to do one in 1979 for Anglia Television, and in 1980 Eric made a second one. I used to say to him (no disrespect to Charles):

'Why do you do these films? You don't need to, why do you take on this extra work?'

The answer was that he thoroughly enjoyed himself doing them. They were a different experience, and somehow caught his imagination. So off he went, filming on location for two or three days until his part in the film was finished. A third film was started in the summer of 1982, but it ran into problems and had to be shelved. In 1984 it was resurrected and Eric promised to work a couple of days on location. That was all that was needed. But the dates were set for the week after he died. Sadly, it was never meant to be.

Meanwhile, in summer 1980 Eric the novelist was also hard at work. He had turned his period of convalescence after Harefield to good use by developing a novel, which was eventually published in 1981 under the title *Mr Lonely*. The idea for the book – about a high-living comedian who ends up accidentally stabbing himself to death on the prongs of the Star Award he has just won – had been ticking away in his mind for some time, and when he was forced to take life easy before his operation he decided: right, now was the time to start writing. He was always modest about his writing activities and never called himself an author, which he thought would have been pretentious. He always said he was a 'writer', and when he began the novel he was encouraged by little more than the old adage that everybody has one good book in them.

Of course, Eric was no novice as a scriptwriter. In their radio days he and Ernie wrote scores of scripts, and they continued to do so for their early television shows. Even when they had regular writers working for them they contributed a great deal to producing the final script, and that was how Eric tackled his novel. To his astonishment, he found it remarkably easy. For a long while he had held himself back because he thought book-writing could only be done by people who had had a good education and were good spellers. However, once he gave it a go he was surprised that he could achieve the results he did. Even though he saw that some of the things he wrote were not particularly big on literary merit, the experience of writing *Mr Lonely* whetted his appetite for more. He wrote two vampire books for children, and was working on a second novel, *Stella*, at the time of his death.

I don't think that writing novels and stories would ever have taken over as *the* front-line activity for Eric, but like his favourite hobby of fishing it gave him enormous pleasure. And, I'm glad to say, others shared in this pleasure. I recently had two letters from schoolteachers who said they had thoroughly enjoyed using *The Reluctant Vampire* in the classroom. The pupils at one of the schools adapted the book into a musical play and it was so popular when they performed it at school that they later gave another performance at a local hall.

In Germany and Denmark, where Morecambe and Wise the performers are virtually unknown, *The Reluctant Vampire* has been translated and published in foreign-language editions. This happened before Eric died, and I know it gave him special delight, because it meant that his German and Danish readers regarded him on his merits as a storyteller (or author) and not as a comedian-turned-writer.

The news that Eric's book was to be published in Germany had a funny side, too. The action takes place in traditional vampire country, in the tiny mid-European land of Gotcha, ruled by King Victor the First, who speaks in a comic German accent. 'Gutt evenink,' he says, in a typical scene, 'I vould like a drink, mine host. A drink out of mine special bottle, ya?' Quite what the German translator made of King Victor's lines we never knew, but we hoped he enjoyed himself!

In September 1980 Eric and I went to Marbella for a holiday. We had a wonderfully relaxing time in a superb hotel, and it was so good to get away from home for a while, and to be away from the telephone and the constant requests to do this or that. There is no doubt that being away did us both a lot of good. However quietly we might try to live at home, we were too accessible to have very much privacy.

The following month we were back in the heart of our family for a very happy occasion, the wedding of Gary and Tracey, followed soon after by the christening of Adam, Gail's baby boy and our second grandchild. In fact, as I now look at my diary for that year, I can see that life in that period was decidedly hectic. How about this for a typical week in the year when you thought you were taking things easy:

Saturday To Royal Lancaster Hotel in London to support function for Harefield Heart Transplants.

Sunday Christening of Adam at St John's Church, Harpenden, and big family get-together at the house.

Monday Lord's Taverners' Ball.

Tuesday Eric to Teddington all day for TV rehearsals.

Wednesday Eric does cover photo sessions for *TV Times*.

And so on. No wonder we felt relaxed when we *did* get away for a holiday break! A little while later, in another sequence of days and nights, we went one November evening to a small dinner party at David McNee's house. Next day, Eric started rehearsing for the Christmas Show. The day after that, he was also at rehearsals and then in the evening he was at the Ritz Casino for a Royal fund-raising dinner, a function he supported at least two years running; it was a stag night, though I was also asked to go along and had dinner separately with a ladies' group. The following day Eric worked on the show, and again on the Thursday; that evening we went to the Royal Albert Hall for the Miss World Contest which Eric was helping to judge. We both of us enjoyed these evenings out, but since most functions go on until two in the morning, and then you have to allow an hour for getting home, it all amounts to a hectic schedule whatever your state of health, and there is no way that you can go on doing it indefinitely and expect to get up early next morning and feel fresh for a day's creative work at the studio.

Also at that time we had to contend with the drama of Steven and the 10p piece that he swallowed! This adventure began at school

LEFT Eric enjoying the sun and fresh air at our villa in Portugal – but not able to resist typing a chapter or two for his book.

RIGHT A beautiful wedding and a beautiful bride. Gary and Tracey leaving the church with Eric getting in on the act!
BELOW One of the rare occasions we went to Silverstone Races to watch Graham Hill. Fooling around with Eric's glasses created a little light relief before the drama of the race.

where Steven, for no very good reason, was balancing a 10p coin on his tongue when a friend slapped him on the back and down it went. The coin stayed out of sight, but definitely somewhere inside Steven, for days.

The school sent him to hospital for an X-ray and it was decided that, short of an operation, nothing was going to shift the coin. As the term was about to end and Steven would be coming home for the Christmas holidays, it was decided to postpone any action until then. All my home-remedy efforts seemed to no avail – large portions of hot porridge oats and doses of liquid paraffin had no effect. After yet another X-ray, the doctor pronounced the coin firmly embedded and, like it or not, Steven was booked into the Middlesex Hospital. This was just two days before Christmas, and Eric and I escorted a very worried young man to his hospital bed. Having spent a little time in the ward consoling him, and of course talking to everyone else, we finally, reluctantly, left.

On our way home, feeling rather miserable about the whole affair, we stopped off to visit my mother. We had a cup of tea and a chat, and before continuing our journey home decided to phone the hospital just to make sure Steven was all right.

The voice at the other end of the line said: 'I'm so glad you've rung, just as we were going to operate we took another X-ray. The coin has gone, so can you please come and collect him!'

A month later, completely on a whim, we bought a property in Florida. At the time it struck me as a very strange thing to be doing – but let the events speak for themselves. Eric and I flew out there on 29 January for a holiday, and stayed in Palm Beach at the Breakers Hotel – a lovely, grandiose type of hotel with magnificent ceilings, the kind of place it would cost far too much to build today. This was at the time when the pound was very high against the dollar, making both property and holidays in the USA suddenly seem very inexpensive and attractive. Eric and I had talked a little bit about buying a place, mainly as an investment – and several of our friends had already taken the plunge – but the cautious side of my nature kept saying yes, that's all very well, but Florida is such a long way away. Owning property abroad is always a worry, as I knew from our villa in Portugal. At least the Algarve was only two and a half hours' flying time from London, whereas Florida was more like seven or eight hours. So we talked it through before we set off on our holiday and agreed that we wouldn't be buying a property out there.

While we were in Palm Beach we looked in the windows of real-estate offices, as most holidaymakers do, just out of interest. Then we got talking to an American lady, Eunice, who worked for a real-estate company. She was very smartly dressed and in her early sixties and a great character who never stopped talking and wrote music as a hobby and played the piano.

'You know,' she said, 'we have an apartment available in my block. And my block is the greatest place. I would *not* live anywhere else. You want to see it? I can take you round there. Come and see for yourself.'

We thought: why not? On the way there, in between serenading us with her latest song, she explained that the apartment, or condominium, was fully furnished down to the last detail, and that included the face flannels. We arrived and were shown in.

It was spacious, comfortable, and spic-and-span modern with white floors and blue and white decor in the main room. Eric looked quickly round, and to my utter amazement I heard him say:

'Oh, this is mine. I'm having this.'

I was dumbfounded, but from the moment he set eyes on that apartment, Eric was determined to have it. What could I say? He was so enthusiastic, I hadn't the heart to throw cold water on the idea, or remind him of our earlier agreement not to saddle ourselves with another property abroad.

We probably paid too much for it, almost the asking price, and from that moment the holiday was clouded for me. When we got home Eric was exhausted from the trans-Atlantic journey and went straight to bed, leaving me to go down to the bank straight away to start organizing the transfer of money and all the other financial and legal details. I found myself thinking: 'This is madness. Why ever am I doing it?' And yet, another part of me wanted to take Eric's side. If he was so keen, why should I get all worked up and try to change his mind? I suppressed my anti-feelings, and the deal went through.

Every year, in what transpired to be the short time left to us, we went to Florida. Eric loved it, and used the apartment as a bolt-hole

Gary couldn't resist taking this photo of Eric in Florida and we now have it framed to add to the collection on the piano.

to get on with his writing. On our first trip there as owners he bought a typewriter; I sat outdoors in the sun, while Eric tapped away indoors on his latest book. He loved it; he loved the change, the climate of Florida, the cleanliness of Palm Beach and the efficient way people ran things there, plus the fact that although he was living among

English-speaking people, he was seldom recognized unless by tourists from Britain. In Florida he could be a tourist himself there and go off to Disneyworld and the other attractions, even spend time in the shops (bookshops were what he always headed for first).

In March Eric was busy promoting his novel *Mr Lonely*, which was launched at Hammicks bookshop in the new Covent Garden piazza. Also in London he did a signing session at Hatchards, a radio interview on the John Dunn show and another for television with Mavis Nicholson – a programme on which, ironically, I have since appeared. Out of London he did further signings in Bristol, Birmingham, Manchester and Leeds. He worked hard to give his first book a good send-off.

Dotted through Eric's career were the awards ceremonies at which he and Ernie were honoured by their colleagues and by various organizations. In 1981 they were voted into the TV Hall of Fame, an award run by the *TV Times*. I look back on these occasions with great pleasure, though some proved more memorable than expected.

Eric and Ernie's very first award was made to them on the day President Kennedy was assassinated. I remember being in a large room at, I think, the Grosvenor House, when whispers began to circulate: 'President Kennedy's been shot', 'Assassinated – Kennedy', 'Kennedy's dead' ... and so on until they took over everyone's attention and, obviously, put a bit of a damper on the awards ceremony.

This was no more than a very unfortunate coincidence. The following year, Kenneth Horne collapsed and died while making an awards speech and we began to think there was a jinx on these occasions, but luckily the sequence of misfortune ended there.

Television work continued more or less all the time in 1981, as the boys steadily worked their way through a complete series, but perhaps the big highlight for us was a special holiday to the United States. We had already made plans to go and then discovered that Louis Benjamin, who now runs the Stoll-Moss Theatres, was also making the trip with his wife. Our friendship with Louis goes back many, many years to Morecambe, where at one time he managed the theatre. These days he goes backwards and forwards to the US like other people catch trains to London. Our idea was to go to New

York, see some of the shows, then travel on to Las Vegas and see some more. It would be refreshing for Eric to see a lot of different acts, and if he collected some new ideas for the M & W Shows, so much the better.

When he heard of our plans, Louis went out of his way to make sure we had a marvellous time. He organized all the booking of theatre seats for us, fixed up our hotel accommodation in Las Vegas, and in general looked after us beautifully. The hospitality we received from Louis and our many American hosts was absolutely wonderful. We went there to see, and we saw ... everything. We saw some great acts, and Eric came home feeling not only shattered from the pace of the trip but also full of ideas. Most of them he couldn't use, unfortunately, because they included some incredible animal acts which, however much he might have wanted them on the Christmas Show, were ruled out by the quarantine laws.

Louis Benjamin knew just about everyone. Among the stars we saw was Liberace on the night he opened at the Hilton Hotel, and this led to an invitation to Liberace's house in Las Vegas – for tea, since he decided he would entertain us in the English style. But when we arrived at his lavish mansion filled with piano-shaped everythings, there was not a teapot in sight. Instead, at five in the afternoon, we were offered gigantic gins! A memorable day, and I never found out whether Liberace really thought that we English only invented tea-time as a kind of alcoholic bridge joining lunch to the cocktail hour.

A few weeks later, Liberace came to this country to appear at the London Palladium. We had said that we looked forward to seeing his show again, and then someone in his entourage contacted us and suggested a date, which happened to be my mother's birthday. Now, it also happens that my mother is a great Liberace fan. When I told them this they said: 'Oh, but you *must* bring your mother.' So we did, and she had a marvellous time. The show was great, and afterwards we went backstage. As if it wasn't thrill enough for my mother to meet Liberace, the press were there too and photographs of their meeting appeared in the newspapers the next day.

In due course Eric and Ernie finished their contract with Thames Television, and they arranged to have a meeting with the top light entertainment planners to sort out the future of Morecambe and

Wise. I knew that Eric had been weighing the pros and cons of what he should do for the best and had tormented himself greatly over it. Sometimes it is the hardest thing in the world to make a decision. He wanted to be fair to himself and not put his health in jeopardy, but he didn't want to throw in his hand if he was fit enough to carry on working – after all, he was only in his fifties. He knew also that whatever he decided for himself affected other people including, of course, Ernie. After a great deal of thought he decided that no, he wouldn't work. This didn't mean total retirement: what he had in mind was a kind of sabbatical, a year off from all heavy commitments, the heaviest of which were the Morecambe and Wise Shows.

He announced his decision to me on the morning of the meeting at Thames Television. Off he went, leaving me to ponder what it would really be like to have Eric at home more or less all the time. Certainly I knew he had lots of plans to do other things. He had his writing to carry on with, he had his fishing, and I knew he wanted to travel . . .

That evening Eric came home relaxed and smiling, and I asked him how the meeting had gone.

'Great,' he said. 'Great. We've signed a marvellous contract for the next three years. We'll do a series, plus a Christmas special, and we're going to do some chat-shows as well.'

I couldn't believe my ears. I said: 'But you left the house convinced that you were going to cut right back. And you were going to take a sabbatical before you did anything else.'

He looked quite hurt. He said: 'I thought you'd be pleased.'

I replied: 'Well, yes. Lovely. But, you know, it is confusing. You did leave saying you were cutting right back. And now you've come back with all this. I mean, you do realize, don't you, that you've just doubled your responsibility.'

Perhaps it was the euphoria of meeting up with friends. I knew the executives at Thames, and I knew them as very pleasant people. They and the boys had obviously had a good talk, and a good lunch, and everything had been amiable and lovely. At such moments it all *sounds* so easy: you'll do a series, then a special, then a chat show, then another series . . . It's all right when you are talking about it. The crunch comes several weeks later when you've got it all to do,

when the shows have to be worked out, learnt and performed, and you've got to be fit – no falling by the wayside.

Since the Harefield operation, and as Eric grew older – or, as he put it, 'Now that I am as old as a can of beans' – his state of health needed careful watching. He was inclined to put on more weight than was good for him, and this was a cause for concern. There were no great bouts of self-indulgence, he was just one of those people who need only a few big meals, plus a few drinks, and the weight starts to go on, and in a short time he would be visibly thicker around the waist and fleshier under the chin. Given all the functions he attended, it was almost inevitable that this would happen from time to time although for the most part he was very sensible about his diet.

At Christmas he always broke the rules, but Christmas was always a big event in our family with about fourteen round the table and Eric at the head. He loved it, and before we sat down to our main meal he would be Father Christmas and hand out the presents. No-one else was allowed to be Father Christmas; it was an inflexible family ritual. Because several of my family are in the hotel trade, and had to work on Christmas morning, we wouldn't finally sit down to dinner until about four in the afternoon. By then the children would have burst with impatience if they hadn't had their presents, and so Father Christmas's big hour came just before dinner.

When all the festivities were done, the debris cleared away and the cigar box closed for the last time, Eric would hate himself for having been so self-indulgent and would go straight back on a strict diet. After Christmas 1983, he was to be especially stern with himself and possibly went over the top in his eagerness to lose weight. Also fresh in his memory at that time was the accident he had suffered while making the Christmas Show. He and Ernie were filming a 'Keystone Kops' scene and the script required them to run at a wall. Eric put rather too much realism into it and hit the wall so hard that the impact jolted his heart out of rhythm. It was not a heart attack as such, although nobody was to know that when it happened; and so he was rushed to hospital by ambulance – Kingston Hospital this

OPPOSITE At home after Adam's christening at St John's Church.

time – and rehearsals for the Christmas show came to a grinding halt. Eric stayed in hospital for two nights and although no permanent damage had been done to his heart, the accident seriously undermined his confidence. He had felt so safe since the operation, but now we had an uneasy feeling that he was still vulnerable.

A cosy chat and a little rest on poppa's knee! Four-year-old Amelia and two-year-old Adam.

Naturally there were times when such thoughts depressed him, and my remedy was to try and kid him out of it. 'You'll outlive us all,' I used to say. 'Just look at your life-line.' It was quite true: he had an exceptionally long life-line which stretched all the way down the palm of his hand and halfway round his wrist!

At other times it seemed as though he expected to live for ever. He would talk of retirement and all the things we would do together, and then add: 'I'll try not to get under your feet!'

'Don't worry,' I said, 'you'll be all right. We'll reorganize ourselves. We'll have to because it's going to be different anyway. We won't be doing the same things, and there won't be all that work coming in with the mail and the phone calls. Gradually everything will wind down.'

He accepted that, but from time to time he seemed to have premonitions that it wouldn't turn out as we planned. The previous summer, in July, he and I and a friend of mine called Margaret were sitting in the garden having tea. David Niven had recently died and we were talking about all the attention that his death had received in Britain. We found this a little surprising, because David had lived for so long in Switzerland and in his work had been more a part of the American scene. Obviously, though, he was remembered with a great deal of affection in this country, and many people had flown out to his funeral. As Margaret and I got up from our chairs, and I picked up the tea tray and started indoors, Eric said:

'Of course, *I* won't be here this time next year.'

Margaret and I both rounded on him. 'Don't be so silly,' we said. 'What a silly thing to say.'

He gave a little shrug, and said nothing.

13
'This is Different'

So many people have said to me: 'Eric could never have retired. He could never have given up the business. The way he died – just after finishing a stage show – was the way he would have wanted to go.'

Some years ago it may have been true that he couldn't have given up the business, but I don't think it was right in 1984. Others didn't know Eric as I knew him. They forget that he was getting older and had worked in show business for nearly all his life. He had loved it, but as the years went by, he had much more anxiety over his health and his ability to complete a TV series without problems. By the beginning of 1984 he had reached a stage where he wanted to give it all up. I certainly believe he would never have made another series of Morecambe and Wise Shows. The fun was going out of them and he wanted to stop. Nobody loved life more than Eric, and now he yearned to continue living in good health and not jeopardize his chances for the future.

The details of certain conversations we had in the weeks before he died are engraved on my memory. In one of them he said:

'You know, if I have another heart attack, it'll kill me. And if I do another Morecambe and Wise series, I'll have a heart attack.'

'Well, in that case,' I said, 'you don't do any more shows, do you.'

He had a habit of walking up behind me – say when I was sitting at my dressing table doing my hair – and starting a conversation. One morning he came up to me and said:

'You know, I've really enjoyed this year. I've really enjoyed having a sabbatical.'

The way he suddenly came out with this, from out of the blue, surprised me. He hadn't done any television work since his encounter with the wall a few months previously, and I was pleased that he sounded so content.

'I *am* glad,' I said. 'And, you know, you're only part-way through the year. There's a long way to go yet.'

'Yes,' he said, 'but already I can see I won't have any trouble with retiring. I've got the writing to do, and all the fun shows . . .'

By fun shows he meant the panel games like *What's My Line?* Before he died he was a guest on four of these shows, and he knew that they were something he enjoyed doing and no effort for him. On top of the fun shows he had his fishing to look forward to; that would fill many hours in the summer months. He also wanted to travel, and planned for us to go on a trip together, driving from New England down to Florida – a journey he'd talked of doing for years.

Before his operation in 1979, Eric wrote me a letter which I was to open if he didn't survive. It was sealed, and he kept it in his desk. Later on, when all was well and he had recovered from the operation, he put the letter in the back of his dressing-table drawer.

Only a week before he died, he tidied out these drawers – something he hadn't done for a long time – and came across the letter. I was sitting at my dressing table when he held up the envelope and said:

'Well, we won't be needing this any more.'

He tore it up and took it out to the dustbin. I have since wondered if it wasn't almost an act of defiance – he wanted so much to feel confident about the future. And yet, why should he suddenly start tidying his drawers, and doing other things which could well be described as 'putting his affairs in order'?

Another example had occurred the week previously when we went up to Lancaster. We had accepted to attend a service commemorating the opening of the Methodist Homes for the Aged, which Eric had supported. By setting off early, we allowed ourselves time to go and visit the graves of Eric's parents, Sadie and George, which Eric had said he wanted to do. We tried to look up some of his few remaining relatives in Morecambe, but most were away. Eric went down to the front and bought his favourite Morecambe Bay shrimps from the Trawl Shop, which sells them fresh from the sea. In Lancaster he called at the market and bought black puddings and tasty Lancashire cheese. Perhaps it was coincidence that he should have done all those special things when he had only a matter of days to live, but I find it very strange.

A few weeks earlier, in February, we went to Palm Beach for a holiday at our apartment, and for the first time he wanted only to enjoy the break and didn't do any writing. Instead, we drove up to Orlando on a hectic tour which took in Disneyworld and the Epcot Centre, Sea World, Cypress Gardens, Circus World ... Thinking back to those few days, they were exhausting and I'm not sure now we should have done as much as we did, but we enjoyed it immensely and returned home in March well pleased with ourselves.

During Steven's Easter holidays, I went to Portugal with my mother, Steven and another young lad of Steven's age. Eric was to have come with us but then, for a combination of reasons, he decided to drop out at the last minute. First of all, the flight arrangements had been rather messed about, and instead of flying from Heathrow we were switched to Gatwick which was not nearly so convenient. Moreover, it was a crack-of-dawn departure so we would have to stay overnight in a nearby hotel. None of us relished this new plan, particularly Eric.

Then it occurred to him that trout fishing was due to start, and he decided he would prefer to stay home and fish rather than go off abroad again. The final setback came when Barney, our sixteen-year-old golden retriever, collapsed in the garden with a heart attack and a stroke, and although he survived, thanks to the promptness of the vet, he needed extra care and would obviously be much happier with one of the family in the house.

In the old days I never left Eric on his own for as much as a week. He hated the idea of me not being at home. But in time the pattern changed so that, come Easter, I would go off to Portugal with my mother, Steven and usually some other members of the family, and Eric would stay at home. We got ourselves organized so that he was well looked after in my absence, with someone coming every day to take care of the house, and I stocked up the freezer with things he enjoyed that could easily be warmed up. Often Eric was in any case doing a television show and so was unable to get away, but in that

ABOVE At home in the garden two years ago. Gail came to visit with Amelia and Adam, and Gary joined us with Tracey and their dear little dog Bowler. He has taken up residence with me now as an almost permanent boarder.
RIGHT 5 May 1984 – stepping out to walk from Lancaster Cathedral to the Methodist Home for the elderly, where we had tea and a chat to some of the residents in their own flats.

case he would usually manage to spend a weekend in the country on a fishing trip. Even so, a fortnight was the limit. He never wanted me to be away for more than two weeks.

This time I came back after a fortnight to find a new, trim Eric. Once he was alone in the house he had put himself on a drastic diet – as usual, no half measures for him – and got down to his perfect weight. He hadn't been so slim in years, and he looked marvellous. He was fit, with a good healthy colour, and he had completely given up all those little extras – like a Scotch in the evening, his pipes and cigars – which in moderation helped to relax him. But moderation, as I said earlier, was alien to his nature, and this latest diet was another example of Eric going to extremes.

All the same, he did look well, and we settled down and really enjoyed the next few weeks. It was so pleasant, just being together quietly, with only social, enjoyable functions in the diary and a couple of days booked for fishing, that we began to say: 'Isn't this nice. If this is what it's going to be like in retirement, it'll be lovely.' The only thing that took edge off our pleasure was a sudden health problem.

Eric began to suffer a stomach and chest complaint which was distressing, but at the same time familiar. He had had this problem before, and was reluctant to go to the doctor because he thought nothing would come of it except that he would be given some kind of indigestion tablets which wouldn't do much good. He decided he would have to live with it and hope it cleared up quickly, but it got worse; now he was having breathing difficulties as well, and in the end we did go to the doctor – together. Eric insisted that I went with him. Eric always liked to have a laugh with the doctor, no matter how serious the occasion, and on this visit he walked into the surgery saying: 'Joan and I have come for some advice on family planning.'

The doctor examined him and suggested it could be a hiatus hernia. We rang the local hospital and fixed a date for the X-ray, but it was for days ahead. We had no idea that valuable time was ticking by.

Ironically, Eric had also chosen these weeks to undergo some fairly extensive dental work, which, as circumstances were to prove, was the height of bad timing.

The X-ray was duly taken, and an appointment also arranged for the heart specialist to come to the house and give Eric an ECG examination. This was for the evening of 25 May, the same day that the X-ray results filtered back to the doctor; these proved negative, which meant there was no hiatus hernia. It was all coming together, but vital time had passed.

We had a wedding to go to the very next day, and a theatre date at Tewkesbury the day after, and were loath to cancel either or both unless it was absolutely necessary. On the afternoon of the twenty-fifth, it seemed as though we would have to cancel, because Eric was not well and couldn't have coped. However, the visit from the specialist changed matters. Some different pills were prescribed and from the first dose Eric improved dramatically.

In the last few weeks of his life, Eric did one or two things that were uncharacteristic of him. One particular incident was when he lost his temper with the press – the only time I've known this to happen. Over the years Eric was wonderful value for the press, and by and large they have appreciated the immense trouble he took, in live interviews or on the phone, to give them good pictures and funny lines. To go further, I would say there was a special friendship between Eric and the press people. He recognized that they had a job to do, and he always put himself out to give them the quick gag and the quotable quote.

When I came back from Portugal I was surprised to find him very upset about a piece that had appeared in one of the national dailies. It had quotes in it that were meant to have come from Ernie, and Eric was really bothered about it. He insisted that I should read the article, and I did.

Certain remarks in it were irritating and provocative, but there was nothing *really* to take umbrage over.

Gary felt the same. Quietly he said to me: 'I wonder why Dad's so upset about that piece in the paper, because really it doesn't mean anything.'

Eric had already rung Ernie, and Ernie had assured him that he hadn't said any of the remarks attributed to him. Usually Eric was so tolerant about mistakes and distortions in the press. If ever he was asked about it, he had a stock reply: 'The hardest thing to find is yesterday's newspaper.'

Not this time. For some reason this article mattered to him. A few days later we went to a Royal charity film show in aid of the United Nations Children's fund, and afterwards everyone went on to a club for a buffet supper. Eric and I were among the first to arrive at the club. We went in and were hovering near the buffet table waiting for the rest of the guests to arrive, when a young man, a reporter, came over and introduced himself. It was the worst thing he could have done because, by coincidence, he was from the newspaper that had printed the piece which had upset Eric so much. He quite innocently brought up the subject of the article and began questioning Eric about it.

As soon as Eric heard where the reporter was from, he started tearing him off a strip. In next to no time I found myself holding Eric by the arm and saying: 'Come on, take it easy. It's not him personally, you know ...'

Eric cooled down instantly, but couldn't wait for Ernie to arrive so he could tell him about it. Ernie came into the room and Eric dashed across and started talking to him in a rather animated way about the article and the reporter he'd just been telling off. Soon after Eric died, one of the newspapers stated that Eric and Ernie had been having a big row! This was quite untrue, of course, and in fact we had had a very pleasant evening together, with Eric and Doreen both celebrating their birthdays.

The twenty-sixth of May dawned, the day of the wedding. Eric had had a much better night's sleep and decided there was no reason why we couldn't go. Steven was home for the bank holiday, and Gail, Paul, Gary and Tracey were joining up with us to go off to the wedding together. A very nice family occasion. It was taking place at the church where Gail and Paul had been married, and Amelia christened.

Gail arrived at the house and was appalled at the difference she saw in Eric. She took me to one side saying: 'Whatever has happened to Dad? Last week he looked marvellous and now he looks so drawn.'

I agreed with Gail, but I could at least derive comfort from the fact that he had seen both the doctor and specialist who had found nothing to warrant emergency measures – even though the specialist had been disturbed by Eric's symptoms and very much wanted some fuller, more up-to-date information on him.

'Why don't you get yourself over to Harefield as soon as possible,' he suggested. 'Go there and let them X-ray your chest and give you all the tests.'

'That's exactly what I intend doing,' Eric agreed. 'I've already talked it over with Joan, and as soon as we get this bank holiday done with we'll phone Harefield.'

It would have been no problem. Eric had only to ring up Harefield and they would have told him to come in. Ironically, he had been there only the week before – helping to raise money at their annual carnival! He'd spent a very tiring day working in the grounds when really, if we had only known, he should have been inside the hospital as a patient, because by that stage he must have been in the early stages of heart failure. Unfortunately I hadn't been with him that day because I had gone to an event at Steven's school, so I wasn't able to give him any support. When he got back that evening he said to me: 'These charity do's are *exhausting*. In the end I just had to get away, I felt completely knocked out.'

The weather was cruel for the wedding, chilly and with torrential rain falling non-stop, and in the church Eric was icy-cold. After the service we had to wait around for a while until someone very kindly rescued the guests by urging them to go on to the reception and leave the wedding group to struggle on as best they could with the photographs. At the reception Eric seemed fine; it was a lovely occasion and he thoroughly enjoyed himself. We left soon after the speeches so that he could get an early night in preparation for the journey to Tewkesbury.

Eric had been invited there by our old friend Stan Stennett, who leases the Roses Theatre from the local council, and he would have hated to let him down. All the same, Eric was sensible about his health. If he had thought there was something seriously wrong, no matter how much this meant disappointing people, he would have said he was terribly sorry but he couldn't appear.

Only weeks before, he had been deeply disturbed when Tommy Cooper had collapsed suddenly on a live TV show and died in front of millions of viewers. This had happened while I was in Portugal, and knowing that Eric would be upset, I had telephoned him. He was very sad and thought it was so awful that Tommy should have died in that way – doing the jokes, then collapsing in front of everyone. He told me he had no intention of taking the same sort of risk himself. Now, on 27 May, although warning bells were sounding in his head and he was keen to get to Harefield the following week, neither he nor I dreamed that he should never have tried to fulfil this date at the Roses Theatre. He had got out of bed that morning saying: 'I feel great – I've had a marvellous night's sleep – why didn't they give me those pills before?'

In the car going to Tewkesbury, Eric looked out at the pouring rain and said:

'I'm glad we didn't go to Blenheim for the Taverners match. It's bound to be rained off.'

It was rare for us to miss the Blenheim match but, as I have mentioned, it slipped our memory that year and we hadn't made room for it in the diary. Eric didn't mind – you can't do everything, after all, and now he looked forward to a fun evening doing a chat show with Stan in a nice little theatre in the country.

In a way the Tewkesbury show was an experiment: Eric wanted to see whether the audience would accept him doing this kind of show – basically an ad-lib conversation – as entertainment. If they did, he planned to do the same sort of thing in retirement.

Already he had his writing and his hobbies, but he needed something else. If all went well, chat shows would be the answer. It wouldn't be for the money, just for the fun and satisfaction he would get from them. What he wanted to do was to make occasional one-night appearances at various small theatres, and perhaps universities, around the country. Many years before, he had done a question-and-answer show at St Albans College which lasted for about an hour and a half and had been extremely well received. He also did a chat show at Haberdashers' Aske's School in Elstree, and the idea for his Tewkesbury appearance stemmed from those earlier performances.

So, as we drove into Gloucestershire, Eric was in high spirits looking forward to the whole weekend. He didn't think that doing something he would enjoy could possibly do him any harm. Unlike working on TV, which was a strain, he felt perfectly relaxed at the prospect of this smaller, more intimate type of entertainment.

I had questioned this and I said: 'Well, even if you're going to enjoy it, you're still going to manufacture an awful lot of adrenalin appearing on stage for an hour or more doing a chat show off the top of your head.'

'Oh,' he said, 'this is different. It's not like television. There's no strain with this. You know me, love. I'll enjoy it.

Looking back, I feel there was nothing wrong with this way of thinking, but we were perhaps naïve not to realize for ourselves that Eric's heart had deteriorated alarmingly, and in a very short space of time. It's so easy to be wise in hindsight.

Eric's confidence in this new style of show was quite justified. He was on top form in the little theatre in Tewkesbury, and the audience thoroughly enjoyed themselves.

They had made quite an occasion of it. The Mayor and town councillors sat in the stalls and the theatre was packed. Eric sat on a chair on stage, with Stan alongside to feed him the occasional line. The chat show occupied the second half of the evening, following a first half of variety. Eric spoke about all sorts of things, even periods from his life that he rarely mentioned, like his time down the mines as a Bevin Boy during the war. This may not have been an electrifying topic in itself, but Eric was constantly throwing in jokes to keep it light and the audience was hanging on to every word. He spoke about the early days – doing pantomime with Stan and the tricks they played on each other. He even talked about Tommy Cooper and the tragic way he had died.

As he went on, his voice grew hoarser, and he kept drinking glasses of water. He'd had this hoarseness for some while, but it bothered me how often he was having to replenish his glass to try and clear his throat.

At the end of the chat session, he asked if anyone had any questions they wanted to ask. He and Ernie had done this at the end of their concerts, and it always seemed to go down well. The questions were light-hearted, on the lines of 'Does Ernie really wear a wig?' At Tewkesbury the questions veered towards the serious, with someone asking for advice about how youngsters could get into show business and how difficult it was now. I could see Eric growing irritated as he tried to put things back on a more humorous level, not wanting to end on a 'low' but on a 'high'. I could tell that he now wanted to finish and leave the stage. At last the right moment arrived and he said his goodnights. Then – the most natural thing in the world – the musicians came back on and picked up their instruments. Eric joined up with them, and in no time at all it developed into a hilarious bit of nonsense with Eric playing away at the vibraphone, with the sticks flying off into the audience. Then he sat down at the piano and did a spot of his unique 'out of tune' playing. In a very short time the act had gone from a calm chat show to a slice of pure music hall – wild, noisy, and energetic.

As he finished on one of the instruments Eric stood and received the audience's applause. They kept wanting him to go on and take more bows. A big drum was thrust in his arms. He disposed of the drum fairly quickly and took his very last curtain-call. Someone in the show wrote me a letter to explain what happened next.

Eric came off the stage saying 'That's your lot' and he walked towards the people watching from the wings. Suddenly he pitched forward and fell, hitting his head on the floor. He lay completely still.

Out in the audience everyone was still clapping, and Stan and the other acts and the musicians were taking their bows, when someone rushed out from the wings shouting: 'Is there a doctor in the house?'

I knew instantly. I was sitting next to Betty Stennett and she looked at me and said: 'Oh, my God!'

I rushed on to the stage and into the wings and there was Eric, laid out on the floor, his face deathly white.

In no time at all, help was beside me. Miraculously, the Mayor of Tewkesbury was a doctor, his wife was a nurse, and there were other nurses in their theatre party. They were marvellous. They did everything at top speed. Eric would have died there and then but for the emergency treatment they gave him, which brought him back from the very edge and kept him going. Within minutes, an ambulance had arrived. The crew were trained in coronary care and they had the right equipment with them, notably the electric pads which are placed over the heart to give it a jolt and restore its rhythm.

We dashed to Cheltenham – a nightmare journey with me sitting in the front with the driver and the doctor and the ambulance men keeping Eric alive in the back. At the hospital they were ready for us. They weren't busy, and in Emergency there didn't seem to be any other heart cases. I sat in a little room and waited while they worked on Eric, and after a long time they brought me in to sit with him.

Eric was unconscious, but clearly struggling to come out of it. He had a breathing tube in his mouth which was giving him quite a bit of difficulty and every now and then he would half choke on it. His heart beats were monitored on a TV screen near the bed.

At first I sat there quietly, holding his hand and watching, then a nurse said: 'Let's try and bring him out of it. Speak to him loudly, as sharp as you like.'

We started calling: 'Eric! Eric! Can you hear us?'

Suddenly he clenched our hands! Afterwards I almost wished he hadn't. I'd like to think that he wasn't aware of all that had happened. He hadn't the strength to somehow heave himself out of the blackness and back to consciousness, but he squeezed our hands with real force.

I thought, thank God, he's going to make it. He'll get better. Then suddenly something happened. I didn't see it on the screen, but it was a crisis. Four of the nursing staff were instantly there. Someone rushed me out and virtually pushed me into a side room, then went back to Eric.

I'm not sure how long I waited there – ten, fifteen, twenty minutes. Then a group of white-clad figures came through the doorway. Their faces said it all. The doctor said:

'We're terribly sorry, Mrs Morecambe, we couldn't save your husband – I'm afraid he's dead. His heart just couldn't take any more.'

14
No Long Faces

I sat in the car being driven home; on the back seat was a carrier bag with some clothes in it which the sister had handed to me as I left the hospital. Our driver, Michael, had collected our case and other belongings from the hotel room which Eric and I never did sleep in. It was the bridal suite, with a large four-poster bed in it, and only a few hours before Eric had joked with me saying:

'You've waited a long time for a honeymoon but at last you're having one!'

In the hospital they had been very kind; they'd asked me if I had any questions. I couldn't think of any at the time; I simply couldn't believe that it was all really happening.

Eric had hung on until four o'clock in the morning; five and a half hours since the fatal attack. There was nothing more that could have been done for him. Many people had done their utmost to save him and it was no-one's fault that their efforts had failed. The mistake was in ever going there . . .

On the car radio a voice said: 'Eric Morecambe died this morning.'

I will always reproach myself for not seeing that he went to Harefield. If he had gone to see Magdi Yacoub, there is no way that he would have been allowed to go to Tewkesbury. He would have needed prolonged treatment, perhaps even a heart transplant, but I do believe that he would have lived.

In the days that followed, I received a letter from Magdi. He was shocked by Eric's death. Later when I saw him he wanted to know exactly what had happened.

'When did Eric actually die?' he asked me.

'Just before four o'clock,' I replied.

'He lived till then?' said Magdi, obviously surprised.

'Yes.'

'Why ever didn't you send for me?'

It took the wind right out of my sails. The appalling thought went through my mind: had I really done everything I could? But ... I would never have thought of sending for this marvellous surgeon who at the time could have been anywhere in the world. On the other hand, the more I considered it, the more it seemed possible. Magdi, being the man that he is – larger than life – could well have made it happen. If I'd rung Harefield, someone would have bleeped him and in no time he'd have been in a helicopter, landing in the grounds of the hospital! It wasn't so fanciful. I thought: 'Dammit. I could have done that.'

The reality, of course, is different. You see that your husband is being urgently cared for in a proper coronary unit, and you don't think that there is anything more you can do. I'm not saying that Magdi could have worked wonders, but I wish I'd thought of asking him.

When I got home to Harpenden it was to find that Gary and Tracey, who had been staying for the weekend in order to look after Steven, had been joined by Gail and Paul. They had driven over as soon as the news was broken to them, and they were all there waiting for me to arrive. Everyone was stunned and, like me, couldn't believe that it was all really happening. To avoid the long lenses of the press now gathering outside, we went into the dining room at the back of the house.

Fiona Castle, Roy's wife, dashed over from where she lived. She meant just to put a letter through the door saying she was there if we needed her. But when we saw her we grabbed her.

'Oh,' she said, 'I can't impose on you now.'

'Yes, you can,' we said. 'You're as good as one of the family.'

She came inside, and I told her some of the details of the last few days. After quietly listening to my story, she said: 'Joan, just one word of advice. Beware of the if-onlys.'

It was true. I was full of them. If only he'd gone to Harefield; if only he hadn't worked; it only he'd retired soon after his operation;

if only I hadn't gone to Portugal and left him by himself...

Fiona is a very caring lady, and she knows what people go through when they are in a state of shock and grief. She was quite right to warn me. She also said: 'Think positive'. This was another good piece of advice, because in the weeks and months to come there were many occasions when I was to find myself dithering and not wanting to make decisions.

Decisions. At no time in my life had I ever been faced with so many. Already, only hours after Eric's death, it had become clear that we were at the centre of a national event. There was no escaping the enormous attention focussed on us, not only by the press and television, but by show-business and family friends, by the local people of Harpenden, and by people everywhere who knew Eric from television and looked upon him as 'one of the family'. Eric was loved by thousands of people who would have been most unhappy to let him go without saying goodbye properly. Any thoughts I may have had of holding a quiet funeral, possible followed some weeks later by a memorial service, had to be quickly set aside.

After giving it a lot of thought, I decided that the funeral should be in Harpenden, at the Church of St Nicholas. Would it be large enough? It was larger than most churches, I was assured, and extra chairs could be brought in. Eric was very much a part of Harpenden life, and I am sure it would have offended a lot of people in our adopted home town if I had taken the funeral elsewhere. The enormous number of people who came and stood outside the church to hear the service relayed to them made me feel quite certain I had done the right thing.

Once the church was chosen, it was a question of who should read the lessons and give the address. I rang Billy Marsh, Eric's agent, who was also a great friend to us over the years. I asked if he could get in touch with Dickie Henderson to see if he would be willing to speak at the service. I knew Eric thought that Dickie was fantastic, and that he had given a marvellous address at the memorial service to Arthur Askey, which had prompted Eric to write Dickie a very funny letter. However, I wasn't thinking quite straight because there is a very big difference between a memorial service and a funeral. Dickie pointed this out to me but said he would be honoured to speak at the funeral and on the day he managed to steer exactly the right middle course. He made us laugh and yet it was all very respectful. The humour basically stemmed from Eric, and the letter he had written him. Dickie quoted from it:

'Your tribute to Arthur reminded us all what a great comedian he was. I should like to book you for my funeral just to remind everyone what a great comic I was.

P.S. I'll pay you when I see you – down there.'

The other speakers at the service were Ernie and Roy Castle, who read the lessons, and the vicar from St John's, the Rev. Gordon Martin, who paid tribute to Eric's work in the local community, especially with sick children.

It was a beautiful service, and my other abiding memory is of the wonderful flowers. Some of the larger and more ornate designs were complete showpieces. In a way it is unfair to single out the spectacular ones because I feel an equal gratitude to everyone who remembered us on that day, whether they sent flowers or wrote us a letter or simply prayed for us. But the flowers were magnificent. So many people had wanted to make that gesture, attaching a card whose constant message was: 'Thank you for the sunshine.'

Luton Town Football Club sent a floral replica of their playing field, complete with players and goals, and the Lord's Taverners sent a lovely arrangement with a cricket bat in flowers, and there were gorgeous arrangements of roses, but the design that drew the most attention was the simplest. 'Where have they come from?' asked the local florists when they saw the huge cascade of sweet peas – flowers that everyone thought were impossible to get at that time of year. Had they been imported? We never knew. They came from Benny Hill, who may have sent them over from France though I've never had a chance to ask him. All anyone can remember is that they arrived in a van driven by an elderly lady, who delivered them at the church and promptly drove off again.

These wonderful sweet peas were one of the centrepieces of a special display put on at the church after the funeral. Some of the flowers were destined to go to a local home and to various hospitals, but for two days they were to remain in the church so that people could come in and see them. To begin with the vicar was worried that they would be left there too long; he wanted to make quite sure I understood that they would be taken away after two days or they would interfere with the normal running of the church.

I assured him that we wouldn't let him down, and two days after the funeral I went to the church in a van with the funeral directors, all set to remove the flowers.

'Oh, no, you can't possible take them now,' said the vicar when he saw us coming. He pointed. 'Look at all these people.'

There was a great queue of people filing into the church. Some of them, we found, had driven from long distances to be there. So I went home without any flowers. Two days later we tried again: same thing. The flowers had become a great focus of interest and still people were coming to pay their respects to Eric. After the initial surprise, I found this very rewarding, and I know Eric would never have dreamt that his funeral would arouse so much interest and sympathy.

After the funeral itself, I went on with the family to a private cremation service at Garston. With me were just close members of the family – Gail and her husband Paul, Gary and his wife Tracey, my mother, my brother Alan and his wife Pam and their three sons, and George and Joanne my uncle and aunt. It had long been Eric's wish to be cremated when he died, and later we were able to bring his ashes back to the church in Harpenden, where they are now buried in the Garden of Remembrance.

Eric always loved the roses in our garden. As soon as the first rose came into bloom, he would sneak out and snip it off and put it in his buttonhole. I used to tell him off about this. In 1984, it so happened that on the day of the funeral the roses were starting to bloom, and when we later had a small private ceremony to bury his ashes, I placed the first rose from our garden on Eric's little plot of ground. This year I took a rose to the Garden of Remembrance on the anniversary of his death, and I hope to do this every year.

OPPOSITE The beginning of a memorable evening. Bryan Cowgill, Louis Benjamin and I greet Prince Philip as he arrives at the London Palladium for Thames Television's tribute to Eric – 'Bring me Sunshine'. Held in aid of the British Heart Foundation, it raised a considerable sum of money for the fund. How proud Eric would have been.

PRIVATE
STALLS

When I looked back over the day, I felt that everything we had done would have met with Eric's approval. This was very important to me: what with Eric being such a stickler for getting things right in his working life, I would have hated for someone to think, 'Oh, no, Eric wouldn't have liked that.' As it was, I felt that it all went off in exactly the way he would have wanted.

Back at the house, tea was being served to a hundred or so friends all crammed together in the living room. It was a fine sunny day and they could have gone out on the terrace or into the garden, but they all seemed to want to crowd together at one end of the room, like the regulars in their favourite pub.

It is strange how at such times of great stress people manage to be so efficient. We didn't bring in any outside caterers, but with the help of good friends and good people who have worked for us over the years, we had everything under control. Cups and saucers, plates, cutlery and glasses – we had them all, a hundred or so of everything, plus piles of sandwiches and cakes, all home-made. In a way, it was probably helpful to have so much to occupy my mind in the week leading up to the funeral. There had been almost no time for private thought.

During that week I surprised myself by the way I kept control of my emotions, and I have carried on doing so when talking about Eric. It's rather out of character – I can cry at a movie on television – but somehow I was able to find a certain inner strength to help me after Eric's death. Even after the funeral I found myself smiling at people. Gail noticed it, and that she was doing the same, and it was she who put it down to the years of 'training', of putting on a good face for the press and the public. Only once did I break down: when the coffin arrived at the church. Instantly the press cameras all went click-click-click; they had been waiting for that moment, the blighters, and that was the lead picture which appeared in many newspapers the following day.

Whenever I did have a spare moment, and during the night, I found my thoughts going immediately to Eric, and I tried to remember his words to me five years before when he was facing up to his operation at Harefield: 'If I go, it's you and the family who will suffer, because you will have to carry on without me. I know you will grieve for me, and I want to be missed and remembered, but I don't want there to be any long faces. If I don't get through this operation, I don't want you to spoil your life because of me.'

I still think of his words and find in them a great source of strength. I miss Eric and remember him all the time, and there is an ache inside me which never quite goes away. But life must go on. There will be long faces, whatever he may have wished, but perhaps in time life will somehow change so that he is not continually in the forefront of my thoughts. That's all I can say.

I am so happy with you
I can discuss all my thoughts, or
I don't have to say anything
You always understand

I am so relaxed with you
I don't need to pretend
I don't need to look good
You accept me for what I am

I am so strong with you
I depend on you for love
but I live my own life
You give me extra confidence
to succeed.

—Susan Polis Schutz

WITH ALL MY LOVE TO
YOU AND 'THE KIDS' – ALL
OF THEM – A BIT SENTIMENTAL
BUT, HELLFIRE – WHY NOT?

LOVE.

Eric

One Year On

When the sad news of their grandfather's death was broken to the children, little Adam, who wasn't then four years old, said: 'Does that mean there won't be any more magic?'

The remark brought tears to our eyes, for although Adam meant it in a quite literal sense, referring to the magic tricks Eric would perform for them, to us it had a much deeper meaning. The magic *was* gone and could never return – only in our thoughts and memories would he remain alive forever.

The very last television performance Eric made will never be shown. It was with Gail and her children in the show called *Whose Baby?* He was proud to appear with them and, of course, Amelia and Adam were bursting for it to be shown on TV.

In some ways this has been the longest year of my life, and yet it has flown. What has filled these past months? I could never have foreseen that it would fall to me to perpetuate the 'Eric Morecambe' name, and yet that is what has happened. There could only be one Eric – no-one could ever fill his shoes – but how satisfying that I should be asked to carry on his name with so many organizations, mainly charitable ones, which he supported. How pleasing that so many people are resolved to keep the name of Eric Morecambe alive.

When Eric was in hospital waiting for his operation, he sent me a card bought from the little shop at Harefield. I have never shown it to anyone, nor did I intend to, but somehow it seems a fitting end to this book. The message inside reads:

WITH ALL MY LOVE TO YOU AND 'THE KIDS' – ALL OF THEM – A BIT SENTIMENTAL BUT, HELLFIRE – WHY NOT? LOVE Eric

Index